Praise for Water Ready

You love rowing, but are you keeping your valuable boats and equipment in their best shape? *Water Ready* is the resource you need right now to keep your rowing trouble-free. Written by two of the most trusted names in the rowing community — Mike Davenport and Margot Zalkind — it has become my troubleshooting go-to!

—Linda Muri, 3-time World Champion,
Gold Medalist Coach, Boat Builder, and Aerospace Engineer

As a USRowing team physician, and a rower, the health and safety of athletes and teammates is always important but is now especially critical secondary to the Covid-19 pandemic.

This book provides very useful and practical information on sanitizing equipment and encouraging athletes to follow simple protocols such as hand washing.

It also reinforces to the readers the importance of a safe environment for the athletes and coaches. Mike and Margot have sensibly covered everything from infection to trailers in an easy-to-read, action-oriented text.

This book is a must-have for anyone involved in rowing: boathouses, clubs, schools, scullers, coaches.

—Jo A. Hannafin, M.D., PH.D.
Professor of Orthopaedic Surgery, Weill Cornell Medical College
Attending Orthopaedic Surgeon and Senior Scientist,
Hospital for Special Surgery
Orthopaedic Director, Women's Sports Medicine Center
Medical Director, HSS Stamford Outpatient Center
Head Team Physician US Rowing
Team Physician, NY Liberty

D1599012

Water Ready is a 'must read' for crew coaches young and old, and a survival guide for anyone in the sport. Mike and Margot are two veteran voices whose collective wisdom has been garnered from decades spent in the sport of rowing.

—Daniel J. Boyne,
Author, *The Red Rose Crew*, Sculler, Coach

Water Ready

How to Get and Keep
Your Rowing Equipment in its Prime

Water Ready

How to Get and Keep
Your Rowing Equipment in its Prime

Michael L. Davenport and Margot Zalkind

The Essential Boathouse Library

Newfane, Vermont

The Essential Boathouse Library
an imprint of
Button Street Press
PO Box 456
Newfane, Vermont 05345
buttonstreetpress.com

Water Ready
How to Get and Keep Your Rowing Equipment in its Prime

Copyright © 2021 Michael L. Davenport and Margot Zalkind

Photos copyright © Michael L. Davenport and Margot Zalkind

Cover photo copyright @ 2019 Caryn Augst

DISCLAIMER

This workbook is designed to provide information in regard to the subject of rowing equipment. It suggests many actions to take for proper care and use of rowing equipment; however, these actions are not and cannot be exhaustive of all necessary actions.

It is not the intent of this workbook to provide all the information that is available concerning rowing equipment. Every effort has been made to make this workbook as complete and as accurate as possible. However, there may be mistakes, both typographical and in content. Do not rely solely on this product for guidance.

The authors, advisors, and publisher shall have neither liability nor responsibility to any person or entity with respect to any loss or damage caused or alleged to be caused directly or indirectly by the information contained in this workbook.

ISBN 978-1-939767-23-3
1st edition

Why This Book Now?

As we write this book (November 2020) we are in a special time.

A pandemic is sweeping the US and the world, and much has changed. We cannot gather in groups for fear of contagion, and like everything else, rowing and racing internationally has been affected by this.

Yes, we do specifically address how to keep your rowers safe, and the virus from spreading. (See Chapter 1.) But our guidelines for rowing equipment are NOT limited to time of a virus.

Winter, bad weather, off times for a school program…there are many times of the year when equipment is lying fallow.

This information is useful to anyone with rowing equipment, any time.

Keep your equipment ready. Always ready.

We strongly advise: Keep your equipment ready.

You train indoors when you cannot be on the water, to maintain race-ready (or row-ready) fitness. Keep your boats and oars similarly poised.

We'll show you how.

MD and MZ

We would like to give special thanks to

Linda Muri
Dr. Jo Hannafin
Dan Boyne
Greg Doyle
Ed Hewitt
Greg Hammond, Concept2
Judy Geer, Concept 2
John Wagner, Washington College
Kari Hughes
Ben Arminger
Caryn Augst
John Geary
Shimano
Jim Pickens
Revolution Rowing
Jim Cooper, Norwalk River Rowing
Doug Lumsden
Space Saver Rowing Systems
Brent Bode
George Kirschbaum
CRI
Lauri Crowe
Dickie Pereli
Inriver Tank and Boat
Joe Racosky
Nielsen-Kellerman

We appreciate all their guidance and wisdom. Any errors are ours.

From the authors: Mike

Havana, Cuba

It was October 1991. I was standing on the bridge of a converted medical ship in the middle of the Gulf of Mexico. We had left Tampa Bay and were on our way to Havana, Cuba.

I stood next to the Captain. The ship, pitching on the waves, was full of supplies and equipment for the Pan American Games, including everything for the US Rowing team. On the top deck of the boat, in hastily built racks, rested our fleet of shells. Our other equipment was spread throughout every possible corner of the ship. Riggers were close to the engine room. Seats were under my bed. And oars were in the hold, the halls, and tied to the racks on the top deck.

I had been selected as Boatman for the US team months before. Now my job was to get all this equipment safely to the course and set up for the team that would arrive in a few weeks. This trip had kept me awake for what seemed like eons.

I was already worried about everything I knew about. Did I have the right riggers? What will get broken (something always does). What if a hurricane decided to roar into the Gulf? But I was freaked out by the unknown.

To start, how would I get the shells down from the top deck of the ship with only a few Cuban rowers to help? How sturdy was the trailer? Who was going to drive? If something broke at the course could I fix it with the tools I had? And what about mosquitos?... gators?...sabotage? At 2:37 am my head would spin out of control with every possible version of disaster.

Two things I've learned about rowing equipment

For more than 40 years, I've been caring for rowing equipment. I've learned a lot and I want to share what I consider two of the most important lessons.

First, rowing equipment is rugged. Sort of. It has an image of being durable, rock solid. And it is—to a point.

The truth is that rowing equipment needs attention. Sure, we can unceremoniously toss riggers into the bottom of a trailer, let large rowers sit in slings, throw wet straps into the dark corner of a boathouse to mold. Trailers can develop wiring problems.

But there is a tipping-point. When that point is reached, riggers break, slings collapse, straps snap, lights malfunction. Then very BAD stuff happens.

Second, there is a relationship between rowing equipment and those who use it—and it's a special one. The trick is to make sure it's positive. For instance, you count on rowing equipment to help you achieve your athletic goals (from sunrise cruises to podium high fives). In turn, your equipment asks only ONE thing from you—that you keep it healthy. If you hold up your end of the bargain, your rowing equipment will be there for you. You fail in your upkeep and so will the equipment.

Up Your Sleeve

It can be overwhelming to throw open a boathouse door and look at all the equipment that needs attention. Having two tricks up your sleeve will help.

First, focus on prevention—keeping issues from happening. Second, the way to do that is by taking little steps, steadily, over time. Do that and you can avoid a multitude of issues. Which means you CAN get and keep your equipment ready for when you need it.

On the following pages you'll find more than 100 preventative actions. These are not vague steps but important details. And not just about rowing shells...they're about ALL the rowing equipment we use, from seats to shoes, bow balls to heel ties, dry rot on trailer tires to backstays, PFDs to electronics. We focus on the important equipment that we depend on for success.

And we'll get into important considerations that often get forgotten—like insurance—which can be disastrous.

How To Use This Book

Using these step-by-step actions will help you get your equipment ready, avoid many issues, and help you be ready to manage misfires if they do happen and there are downloadable checklists of all the actions you need.

As this is being written we are in the midst of a global pandemic. Our rowing world has been put on hold—with more downtime than water time. Things are very quiet which means you should jump on these actions NOW.

However, don't think they can only be done in fallow times— you can do most if not all of them whenever you can, even once the season is in full swing. These actions will make your rowing equipment relationship much better WHENEVER you do them!

Jump right into the actions or chapter that is most relevant to your situation.

Have sling issues? Worried about safety? You'll find actions from me and also from my partner in crime, Margot Zalkind, who you will hear from next. With our years of experience(s) and love of rowing we are creating this to help you to find the success you desire with your rowing equipment.

Back to the Cuba trip

Before I departed for Cuba I finally got fed up with my middle-of-the-night freak outs. So I wrote down every possible issue that I could imagine. Then I recorded step-by-step actions I would take BEFORE the issue came up. And it worked—our Cuba trip rocked. For example, I learned just enough Spanish so I could converse with our Cuban friends who were helping me unload. ("Atento"—careful—was one!) They were amazing, we worked well as a team, and nothing was damaged.

As it turned out, almost all of my late-night what-if scenarios were prevented.

So now to you. Are YOU responsible for rowing equipment (maybe your own or for a huge team)? Do YOU want to avoid issues, and get your equipment ready, regardless of the time of the season you are in? If so, dive into the proactive steps that follow. Pre-planning and taking action make all the difference. It worked for us and it will for you. We are here to help.

It's go time!

Mike Davenport
Explainer, Coach, Boatman

From the authors: Margot

Washington DC 1990s.

The trailer was loaded.

It was dark, late, we were pulling out from the tangle of poles and lights and buildings under the overpass in front of Potomac Boat Club in DC. We had just finished hours of trailer loading, with many hands climbing and strapping and helping.

We inspected our sardine-like placing of interlaced shells, singles slung by straps, hanging down from racks. I recall something like a total of 22 boats and even an erg (we wanted to stay racing-fit after sitting for many hours each travel day).

The gorgeous delicate wooden singles we were taking for Philadelphia scullers were carefully wrapped in layers, so no rubbing could mar their surfaces.

Everything checked:

- Eights on top, fours threaded through the racks.
- Riggers loaded, oars strapped in, seats bungeed in to avoid them slamming about or falling out. We had it covered.
- Red flags hanging down from boats overhanging the rear racks.

We were leaving Potomac Boat Club for Long Beach, California.

We had the weight of the boats and equipment in the bed of the trailer distributed correctly, to avoid fishtailing. Chain hitch was good.

Wiring and tail lights worked.

I checked my travel checklist and it looked great.

Oars, riggers, all labeled, all accounted for.

(Yes, we knew about the four that had arrived at The Head of The Charles Regatta with the wrong riggers.)

Three drivers, a coxswain, and 2 rowers.

And gear packed into every crevice, for all of us and from those who were flying west.
I was feeling okay.
We were on schedule, we had the trip mapped out,
we had playlists loaded, even good snacks.
BUT.

My then brother-in-law, one of our drivers and one of those modest and wonderful people who had careful engineering in his genes, quietly looked over the load, checked straps, added a red flag or two on the overhanging boats.
He then quietly said to me,
"Are you concerned about the sides of those tires?"
I looked. Then everyone looked.
Remember, it was dark, late.
The dry rot on the tires was suddenly visible.
This trailer was a borrowed rig, from a local university.
We needed their extra-large trailer for such a long trip and so many boats.

But,
and here is the point of all of this:
The trailer had been sitting in a field for a long time.
Unused, unnoticed.
Thank goodness he looked, thank goodness he saw.
Blown tires while hauling this load?
In Oklahoma? Or on a busy city beltway?
It was almost easy to miss, but the possible damage?

Our book is full of these points as well as our action lists.
What to look for, and what to keep up-to-date, in usable function.
Our goal? To keep you safe.
To keep your equipment safe.
Whether it is your boat, your seat, your riggers, your oars, or anything you need for rowing happily and safety, we'll cover it.

Of course I added Tire Check to my Trailer Travel Checklist
(we'll get into that in this book).
We arrived in California days later, road-weary but without incident.

We had partaken of too many potato-filled Denny's breakfasts, too many syrup-covered Pancake House meals, too much Mountain Dew. But we got there. And back.

Back? That's another story.

Food poisoning, two drivers disabled and sick, a young enthusiastic coxswain riding shotgun for me and scoping out gas stations... And an abandoned Empacher single hopped a ride east with us. Oh, the rowing stories.

MZ

Chair, USRowing Safety Committee 19 years
Competitive Masters Rower 30 years
Executive Director, Foundation for Rowing Education
(Recipients, Coast Guard Grant for Safe Coxing,
Safe Trailer Driving and Safe Launch Driving education)

Contents

Mike Davenport working on his boat. Note the straps over the boat for stability.

Introduction

You love rowing. It's so simple, right? You take out your boat, you row, you come back, put your boat away, and do it all again the next time. Maybe you stretch on your own because you've heard stretching is good for you. Or you wipe down your boat, if only so it doesn't drip on whatever is under it. Even if you were to take it up a notch - for better technique or fitness, you might work with a coach, get a lesson, hire a nutritionist. But... what are you doing to truly maintain your boat, equipment, etc? Is it enough?

If you have asked yourself any of these questions, you owe it to yourself to read on. Who takes care of your boat? What other equipment do you have? Is there a boathouse? Or maybe you are a coach? What if you are on your own? This book by Mike Davenport and Margot Zalkind will answer your questions. Think of it as your personal boatman.

I've spent years designing and fixing boats, decades racing, and coaching. Time and time again, Mike has been one of my most reliable sources for how-tos and innovations that save me time and money. Margot keeps things real — she knows the real rowers out there and what they want to know. Together, they have saved me hours of worry which meant tomorrow's race outcome was the only thing keeping me awake overnight.

More importantly, this book distills decades of their combined experience on, off, and around the water into a straightforward, no-nonsense approach. As Mike writes, "These are not vague steps but important details." He and Margot outline step-by-step actions to assist you with everything from taking care of your boat and oars, to traveling, and maintaining your equipment in and around your boathouse.

You won't be disappointed with the chapter on boathouse maintenance. This works just as well for the single sculler who cartops out of their home every day: "How Having a Two-Pile System Can Help You Avoid Disaster." Who knew how important it is to get rid of that ragged boat strap or creaky sling? I know how easy it is to think, oh, I'll just use it one more time. Wrong answer. Read on.

When I read this book, I wasn't expecting to come away with a lot of new ideas and methods, but Mike and Margot did not disappoint. I now have a newfound appreciation for Windex (oar handles, anyone).

Don't find yourself stranded. Your boat won't fix itself, oars aren't invincible, and slings DO collapse.

Put away that can of WD-40, wipe out those grimy tracks the right way, quiet that squeaky seat, and prepare yourself for the row of your life.

Linda Muri
3-time World Champion, Gold Medalist Coach
Boat Builder, and Aerospace Engineer

Health and Safety: Germs be Gone

1

These are unusual times.

As we write this, we are in the midst of a worldwide pandemic. It is not the first we have had, it may not be the last. But this tragic experience has brought to the forefront of everyone's consciousness the importance of sane disinfecting and taking unusual steps to stay safe.

Today, more than ever, you MUST incorporate disinfecting the equipment into your rowing-equipment workflow. This is no longer optional.

A confusing part for some is the difference between disinfecting and cleaning. Disinfecting is different from cleaning: Cleaning is for function, for maintenance, for longevity. Disinfecting is for hygiene and health.

What do we mean by "sanely disinfect?"

Let's start with two quick definitions:

- Sanely: with good sense or in a reasonable or intelligent manner
- Disinfect: to free from infection especially by destroying harmful microorganisms

Putting those two definitions together gives us an action plan: a reasonable way to remove or destroy microorganisms.

How to sanely disinfect rowing equipment;

Following are actions to help you disinfect sanely. They are for shared rowing equipment. If you are the only person using the equipment then your disinfecting needs are much simpler than if the equipment is shared. With that written, using any or all of these actions won't hurt if the equipment is not shared. (That's what we mean by sanely.)

Action 1: Wash hands. The split-second people arrive at your rowing facility have them wash their hands. And again as they start to leave. This one action alone is critical. But here's the problem—humans are lousy at washing hands. We forget. (Yes, that includes you and us.) Change that.

How? Maybe you need someone to be a hand-washing leader. Or maybe gentle reminders will work. Or who knows, maybe gamifying it will work, such as washing for 20 seconds with soap and water, getting all parts of the hands and singing Row, Row, Row Your Boat while doing it. Try to identify what works best in your situation, and then do it. And incorporate a good hand sanitizer, too.

Clean it!

Disinfect your equipment like you mean it.

Now on to the equipment...

Disinfect your equipment like you mean it. LIKE-YOUR-NEXT-RACE-DEPENDS-ON-IT. Because it certainly could. How do you disinfect equipment?

A critical component of sane disinfecting is bleach—a diluted solution. Bleach is simple—made from common salt, water and sodium chloride. Bleach is safe when used as directed. And bleach is cheap. Mike has been espousing the power of bleach and disinfecting since the 1990's because he has had too many experiences as a coach and rower of illnesses being "passed around."

Think of it like this, now it's time to go BIG with bleach.

Here are a couple of tricks to using bleach the right way:

- Use a fresh bottle, bleach can lose effectiveness over time (loses about 20% per year.)

- Mix a solution of 1:9 ratio (1 part bleach to 9 parts water). Mix it fresh each day.

- Make a slightly stronger solution if your mixture will sit around for a few days.

Where to disinfect?

There are 8 main areas to focus on for disinfecting rowing equipment:

Action 2: Disinfect oar handles. Oar handles are the most common piece of "shared equipment." Disinfect with a fresh bleach dip AFTER each row.

Concept2 recommends using a bleach solution of 1 cup/5 gallons of water. Mix it up, dip the handles, rinse, let air dry. Make sure you get the entire handle.

Greg Doyle, of Croker Oars USA, has a recommendation— dunk before AND after rowing. According to Greg:

> *For all our grips—foam, timber, or rubber—the post-row dip in 10% bleach solution then rinse clean is ideal to disinfect. But take it up a notch, work with handles that are already clean to start. It would be a good idea to dip and rinse prior to rowing just to be sure someone did not forget after the prior row. Rowers can live with wet handles. It's kind of our thing.*

Action 3: Boat surfaces. Any surface that a rower will touch—seat top, gunwale, oarlock, non-removable shoes— wipe down with disinfecting wipes, or spray with your bleach mix.

Action 4: Indoor rower handles. Follow the previous oar handle recommendations but keep in mind that dipping will probably be awkward. So use a spray bottle of fresh bleach solution—and treat the handles before AND after use. But don't use bleach on the seat rail (it will stain it). According to Concept2 use a cloth or soft scrub pad for that.

Action 5: Seat tops. See "boat surfaces" above.

Action 6: Quick release rowing shoes. If you have quick release footwear, like Shimano Rowing Dynamics, then remove and clean them.

According to John Geary, business manager for Shimano:

> *The crews that use Shimano typically clean and sanitize their shoes by soaking them for a few hours in a five gallon bucket with soapy water (take the insoles out first) and then let them air dry overnight outside in cool dry temps. Or inside in front of a fan. The insoles can go in the dishwasher or regular washing machine. It's the best way to clean/disinfect them without taking the cleats off.*

> *For other shoes, try spraying with bleach solution or another known disinfecting product before and after each row.*

Action 7: Microphones. Here is our suggestion—give each coxswain their own microphone. Just bite the bullet and do it. And do that from now on. The cost is well worth it.

But if the mics have to be shared, then pay attention to this tip from Joe Racosky at Nielsen-Kellerman (makers of the N-K Cox Box):

Purchase a set of 'finger cots' to put on the end of the microphone. These are not hard to find at pharmacies. The finger cot should not affect the overall sound amplification and can be removed after use and then a new one reapplied for the next user.

Action 8: Electronics surfaces (but not microphones). Use the bleach spray at 10% strength.

Action 9: Tools and weights. Bleach will work here, however, bleach shouldn't be applied to copper or stainless steel because it can react with those metals and leave behind stains and even corrosion. If you are unsure and have any questions about disinfecting effectively, contact the equipment manufacturer.

Takeaway

Viruses and other germs can hang out in any area. Luckily you can reduce the possibility of cross-contamination with a proactive, effective and sane plan. You don't need to be fancy, go expensive, or be invasive to sanely disinfect. Using these recommendations you can help rowers, coxswains, and coaches stay safer. All year long. Every year.

2

Boathouse Organization: How a Two-Pile System Can Help You Avoid Disaster

How fit is your rowing equipment?

Do it!
Inspect
your
equipment.

Often rowing equipment will wear out, break, or just become usable. With budgets tight, and equipment getting pushed to the limit it happens more and more. The tough thing is you may not know when that happens to your equipment until it is too late.

That's why we recommend twice-per-season inspections of the equipment—ALL your equipment.

Inspecting the equipment at the beginning AND the end of the season may sound like a lot

Most coaches are pretty good at checking over hulls and oars. However, it's the little stuff that often gets ignored. Which is too bad because the little stuff can have a BIG impact.

Small things like a strap, a sling, a rack, a seat wheel can easily wear out and when that happens that small thing can:

• Stop a practice

• Destroy a boat

• Lose a race

• Injure an athlete

All those have happened to us, from equipment, small pieces of equipment that should have been replaced or repaired early in the process…but maybe we missed them because we did not do our inspections?

Nothing really fancy to this—inspection is a critical part of keeping rowing equipment in good usable condition. And that is our goal.

Margot has seen many boathouses utilize an efficient system regarding equipment and any damage. For example, they use a designated notepad by the log book (or somewhere central) and ask every rower, coxswain, or coach to note any problems they have experienced or seen. Loose rigger? Wobbly seat wheel? Splintery oar handle? Missing hardware? Wiring erratic? Make a note. Don't let it go, don't wait for the next rower or cox to suffer, too.

Do you have a system to address broken equipment? Is there someone knowledgeable in charge of equipment so it is not an "anything goes" system of inexperienced (or ignored) repair?

Who handles this information? If you don't have such a system or person, set up a system. Train someone, and/or locate/identify a good repair person. Many items do not require expertise, just knowledge and the right tools and hardware. And sometimes a replacement wheel or seat or part.

You might find this next system helpful.

Piles! Use a 2-pile system to sort out the good equipment from the bad.

The Two-Pile System

When Mike first started as a boatman, Joe, an old salt of a boatman, took him under his wing. He showed Mike the power of inspection and to use a two-pile system.

Here's how it works.

The GOOD PILE/BAD PILE system

When inspecting equipment, Mike sets up a GOOD PILE and a BAD PILE.

Action 10: The GOOD PILE. In the GOOD PILE is equipment that's ready to go—it's in good or better shape. Something that can be trusted. The BAD PILE is for things that are either in need of repair or need to be replaced. This may sound a bit simplistic, but often equipment gets into a jumble when we're in a rush.

An example: say it is the end of the season and Mike needs to inspect his boat straps. He will put them in the back of his car and take them away from the boathouse (we'll explain why in a moment). In a calm place, where he can focus, he goes through them one-by-one.

Lesson:

Good Pile
KEEP

Bad pile
HEAVE!

Action 11: Protect GOOD PILE from BAD PILE. Then Mike does the most important step of all. He does not, repeat DOES NOT take the BAD PILE back to the boathouse—because bad boat straps are the escape artists of rowing equipment. They WILL end up back in your GOOD PILE. Be careful because that happens all the time.

Takeaway

Simplify, simplify. Be proactive on equipment. A strong system helps avoid mishaps.

The Boathouse Checklist

Things to consider for Boathouse safety, inside and out

Safety in the Boathouse:

- ❑ First Aid Kits
- ❑ Safety poster/reminders
- ❑ Emergency phone contact numbers
- ❑ Land line phone
- ❑ Log book (ELECTRONIC OR PAPER)
- ❑ Book to record all damages/ missing parts

Inside the Boathouse

Look around with a critical eye.

Is there any way someone could get hurt here?

Trip? Bang into something?

- ❑ Sharp edges on racks
- ❑ Slippery, oily floors
- ❑ Rags
- ❑ Riggers on the floor
- ❑ Boats in the aisles
- ❑ Misc. carts, wheels, pontoons, ergs? SPARE PARTS?
- ❑ Bottles, trash, broken glass
- ❑ Nails, screws, bolts on the floor.

Outside

The Docks and Ramps:

- ❑ Check for splintering wood or cracks.
- ❑ Broken wood pieces
- ❑ Anything slippery—
  - ◆ Ice
  - ◆ Bird droppings

- ❏ Moss
- ❏ Any debris:
  - ◆ Trash
  - ◆ Broken glass
  - ◆ Fishing lures, lines and hooks

Fencing/barriers:

- ❏ NB: Your club can be liable if someone accesses your dock and comes to harm. Anyone. Not just members.
- ❏ Keep unattended children, animals, people OFF your dock.
- ❏ Make sure there are sturdy fences or barriers and signage about private property.

Oar Maintenance: Now Is the Perfect Time

3

There are two interesting myths about oars that bounce around boathouses. One goes something like this:

Rowing oars are indestructible. You can run over them with a truck and just keep on rowing.

Nope, they're not indestructible, and we know from experience that if you run over them with a truck that they will break. They also age and with age they can drastically under-perform.

The second myth goes like this:

Rowing oars need more love and care than a parrot

If you've ever had a parrot you know that they are VERY high maintenance. VERY. But again, nope, that myth is false and they are NOT that high maintenance.

The truth is somewhere in the middle. The fact of the matter is that your rowing oars ARE tough but they DO need love, which means you do need to invest in oar maintenance and there are two reasons to take oar maintenance action right now.

First, you want your oars to function as best as they can. Second, during downtime the oars have been sitting—high and dry. And that means it's the perfect time to give them the love they deserve. With that written, let's give your oars the attention they need. But first a word of caution: today's oars are made of materials which could splinter if damaged, and those splinters can be very nasty to hands. Be careful as you proceed!

Myth 1:
Rowing oars don't break. You can run over them with a truck and just keep on rowing.

Myth 2:
Rowing oars need more love and care than a parrot.

Action 12: Start with a handle inspection. Take a set of oars out of the rack and put them on two sawhorses. Go through each handle, whether wood or synthetic.

You are looking for dings, rips, and areas that could be un-kind to a rower's hands. Use a non-permanent marker to cir-cle any spot that needs attention. Second, if you have adjust-able handles, check the fasteners—make sure they are secure.

Action 13: Sleeve and collar inspection. These are sneaky areas because they get a significant amount of wear… second only to the wheels of the seats. It can be easy to overlook issues.

When inspecting keep a keen eye open for areas that are worn or cracked. They might be hard to see but they are indications that the parts need to be replaced. Don't worry about the exact placement of the collar right now—you can adjust that easily later when you have selected your rigging numbers.

Action 14: Inspect the shaft. The shaft starts at the handle, runs under the sleeve and connects to the spoon. It's long and is critical to the oar's function. And it also suffers a lot of abuse.

BE AWARE!

Splintered oars are dangerous to your hands!

Look at the shaft for ding, dents, or breaks in the material. These are signs of damage which can weaken the strength of the oar. Also look for signs of photodegradation—signs that ultraviolet rays are weakening the integrity of the oar. If you see this it is a sign that the oar should be on your replacement list. Marked damaged areas.

Now wiggle the oars—hear any water sloshing inside the shaft? If so, you've got a leak. It might be from a crack or dent you've found or if you didn't find any, then the water in the oar is telling you that there is one. Look again.

Getting the water out of the oar shaft might be a quick fix, such as turning it upside down and letting it drain out if you have an adjustable handle. Or it could be more involved.

Just remember, the water got in there somehow so there is an issue to take care of. We suggest a quick reach out to the manufacturer if you're stuck.

Action 15: Don't ignore the blades. On to the blades (aka spoons). Physically put your hands on each and every blade. (Again, be careful about splinters and broken areas. You may want to wear heavy gloves for this part.) Look for cracks—especially in the tips. Push and squeeze. Any cracks or breaks need to be repaired and, since the oars are probably dry, this would be a great time for those repairs. Mark damaged spots with your marker or tape.

If there are glued tips on the end of the oars (such as Vortex tips) are they secure? Look at the edge for breaks, cracks and splits. Any damaged areas will need to be repaired—pronto. A broken oar can bring a practice to a screeching halt.

Action 16: Sort and fix the oars. Oars that pass inspection with flying colors need to have their handles cleaned and disinfected. Those needing attention go into a repair pile with a note to receive immediate attention.

This one step—labeling any oar and the damaged area clearly so that it's obvious it needs to be repaired—is critical. You'd be surprised how many broken oars end up back in use before repairs can happen, especially in a multi-human boathouse.

Now you've got a pile of oars in need of love. If you are unsure of how to fix them contact the manufacturer. They are the experts at oar maintenance and repair.

Action 17: Cleaning the oar handles. For the ready-to-row oars in your GOOD pile you have one more action to take—clean the handles. The material your handle is made of will determine the best way to clean it.

Today, most (but not all) grips are made of synthetics. There are many different types of materials, sizes, and colors used. Regardless of these differences we found one commonality— if the grip is not clean it can significantly impact the rower's performance. Over time a grip can get dirty with skin, sweat, blood, oil, and plain old dirt. All of these can cover an oar grip with a slippery coating.

Safety!

A clean handle is a safe handle!

To clean a wooden handle (remember, this is *cleaning* not *disinfecting*), water, soap, and a soft wire brush should do.

If you are cleaning a wooden handle (not veneer but solid wood) wash the handle with soap and water and then let dry. Take the wire brush and gently brush the handle from the oar shaft towards the butt of the handle. Try to go 90 degrees to the grain of the wood, but not in the direction of the grain. Once you have gently roughed up the handle, wash again, let dry and you should be fine.

Cleaning a synthetic grip (or a wooden veneer grip) is a little different. Wash the grip with soap and water, and then rinse. Spray with Windex (you can use other cleaners but we've had great success with Windex). Rub well with soft kitchen-type scrubby. Rinse. Let dry. If you want more specifics in cleaning the grips, again, reach out to the manufacturers. In Chapter 1 we discussed disinfecting oar handles, which, again, is different than the cleaning we are doing here.

Takeaway

Oars are often overlooked, when it comes to upkeep. But they are THE point-of-contact for transmission of germs, for blisters, splinters, pain. Coddle them, protect them, and protect your rower's hands.

Slings: Avoid the Big Letdown   4

Nothing is quite as unexpected, ego-busting, and distracting to a rower on race day as a shell crashing to the ground when a boat sling collapses. And few things are more preventable.

Don't skimp on boat slings

Rowing shell slings (aka trestles or portable workstations) are designed to do one thing and to do it well—support the weight of a shell at the proper height so it can be worked on.

Proper height of sling makes working on boat much easier

It's an important challenge and most well-designed slings are up for it—but only if they are in good condition. We've seen too many people put brand new, expensive racing shells in very marginal-quality slings. And we've seen, unfortunately, a dozen times where a marginal sling wasn't up for the challenge and a boat crashed straight down or tipped over. Riggers broke, shell damaged.

What goes into high quality rowing shell slings?

A good quality rowing shell sling:

- Will easily fold, unfold, and fold flat
- Has stainless steel fasteners
- Is weight rated for your equipment (300+ pounds for an 8)
- Is sturdy when boat is loaded
- Made of solid and durable material
- Has a low cradle area (where the hull sits) that is below top parts of sling (helps with balance)
- Holds boat at a height that allows for easy working on boat seats-up or seats-down (24-36 inches tall)
- Lasts a long time

According to Lauri Crowe, President of Suspenz. Inc, maker of a wide variety of slings, racks and workstations, there are a few quality traits to look for:

Simple things are important and a sign of quality such as nut and bolt fasteners (no rivets), thick rubber feet, and tough sling material.

However, regardless of the quality of a rowing sling, there are two issues which will quickly shorten the lifespan and usefulness of any sling.

What destroys a rowing shell sling

First, slings get abused—especially in storage and transport. Piles of slings in the corner of the boathouse or in the bottom of a shell trailer are common sights. That is, if you can see them from all the stuff stacked on top of them.

Second, rowing slings get little if any maintenance—until something bad happens. They are put away wet where their cradle material mildews and rots, or their non-stainless fasteners corrode. By being proactive with your boat sling maintenance you can save yourself a big (crashing) letdown.

Following is a plan to do just that.

Action 18: Inspect the slings. Find an area where you can work. Gather up your slings and prepare for an inspection. Take each sling, set it up, and give it the once over.

If you have folding slings (the most common type) inspect the fasteners at the intersection of the legs. Make sure they are healthy and tight. Next, check the fasteners that hold the cradle material to the legs.

Smarts!
Only use top quality slings. It's your boat,

Check fasteners throughout the sling for health and tightness, and no sharp edges.

Action 19: Inspect the cradle. Now search for frayed or rotten areas in the material that holds the boat. Inspect with care, and look for any areas that show wear. Frayed areas are weak spots and often prone to ripping. As the picture on page 18 shows, small tears can happen and SMALL will become BIG in short order.

Action 20: Repair your boat slings. After inspection, if the sling looks good, put it in a GOOD pile, and move on to the

Ripped cradle fabric can quickly cause issues, it's a warning sign that repairs are needed

next one. If the sling isn't perfect, either repair or recycle it— but make sure you take any steps you need to keep it out of the GOOD pile.

Repairs might be as simple as tightening loose fasteners. Or more involved, like replacing the cradle material, cross member, or legs. If you are unsure how-to or if-you-should repair or replace your boat sling then reach out to the manufacturer.

The price of a new slings could be around $150 a set (or more), YET the price of the boat you want it to safely support is a lot more. So, we'd err on the side of caution and just go ahead and replace the sling if you have any doubts about it.

Action 21: Replacing the slings. If you've decided to go the new-sling-route there are companies that sell-high quality rowing shell slings. We are most comfortable with slings made with aluminum tubing, that have cradles which are deep and made of tough material.

Models such as the "Atlanta sling" are very popular and those are our favorite. What's great about boat slings like those is you can put your boat seats-up or seats-down, and the internal frame is strong and can lock open. They also fold flat and are easy to carry. You can easily put a strap over the boat to secure it while in the sling.

Action 22: Storing your slings. This will take some thought to do properly because how and where you store your slings is going to greatly impact how long they last.

A few recommendations for YOUR sling storage:

- Designate a specific area for sling storage, out of the way, but accessible when needed

- Store slings in upright position (reduces stuff stacked on top of them)

- Pick an area out of direct sunlight, dry and that has decent airflow (cradle material can mildew)

- Identify/label each sling with ownership

Careful!

Store your slings carefully.

Takeaway

Inspect/repair/replace your slings more than once a year. And limit their use to boats, not people, not anything else.

How to kill a sling? Sit on it. In other words, don't.

5   Boat Straps: Do They Hate Us?

Someone has to tell you—your boat straps hate you. And even worse…they will get revenge.

Here's why they hate you: you abuse the heck out of them. You don't give them the time of day. Then you count on them multiple times to make your coaching life easy.

Why your boat straps are important

Quality boat straps (AKA tie downs) are critical in rowing. They help us avoid the 3 Terrible-D's of working with rowing equipment:

- Destruction
- Devastation
- Disaster

Without quality straps YOU are going to have problems—maybe not today, but certainly tomorrow. Unfortunately, it's happened to many, especially Mike. Like the time he destroyed a rowing shell. Crushed it.

He doesn't blame the strap that broke—causing the accident. Instead, he blames himself for mistreating the boat straps and not checking them often for issues. It was a hard lesson to learn. Let's keep that from happening to you.

What goes into high quality boat straps?

When Mike first started rowing, straps were made from cotton webbing. You made loops in it, and tied down the boats. The next version of straps were fancy shock cords (AKA bungee cords).

When you see a nick, toss the strap.

Spiffy but marginal in their use, and SOMEWHAT danger-ous. They stretch and have damaging metal hooks at the end. Not good.

Today, rowing shell straps are much different, and so much better.

What goes into a high quality strap? You want to look for:

- 1" to 2" wide webbing (1" is the most common width)
- Spring loaded cam buckle with stainless-steel springs
- Webbing made of either nylon or polypropylene
- 9' or 12' length (two most common sizes in rowing)
- Minimum Breaking Strength (MBS) of 1,500 lbs
- Strap length indicated on buckle, webbing or with tag
- Protective fabric behind the buckle to protect the boat's surface

Get the best—
You are worth it!

According to Jim Pickens, owner of Revolution Rowing, one area that people overlook in a strap is the stitching.

The stitching secures the webbing to the cam buckle. Substandard stitching or stitching that has been damaged is an accident waiting to happen.

Pickens noted that box-end stitching is the best stitching and a sign of quality. You can get upgrades on straps like having your program's name woven into the webbing or a specific color but the items in the above list are what you should look for.

Keep this in mind—quality boat straps will NOT have straight stitching

What kills boat straps?

There are two main culprits waiting to destroy your straps. The first is ultraviolet rays—they cause photodegradation of the webbing material. You can tell that is happening by feel (webbing will feel powdery) and sight (webbing will start to fray along edges).

Wear is the second culprit that will destroy a strap. The spring in the buckle can break (or get corroded and encrusted)) or the webbing material and cam's teeth get worn enough that the cam won't securely hold the strap. Also, straps can get small cuts that greatly reduce their integrity. Often this is caused by the sharp edges on gunwales or the metal fasteners on boats.

Regardless of cause, a smart person will inspect boat straps before and during the season to make sure the straps will be 100% ready.

Action 23: Inspect the cam buckles. Gather up all of your straps and take them some place away from the boathouse (Yep, it's the two-pile system). Lay out all the straps. Then check the cam buckles to make sure each functions well. Thread the strap end through the buckle—was it hard or easy to thread? Now test the tightness of the grip. Do that by pulling the strap and seeing if it slips in the cam. If it does, even the smallest amount, it's bad.

Check the teeth of the cam and the spring

Put the straps with good cams in a GOOD pile, and whichever aren't top-notch set aside in a BAD pile. Keep these two piles separate.

Action 24: Inspect the strap material. Now take each strap in the GOOD pile, and check through the webbing material. Even though the webbing is made of tough materials like nylon or polypropylene it can degrade. Check all the edges for cuts, frays, shreds, tears, or a feeling of dryness of the material. What's a sign of a bad strap? Cuts, nicks and wear like in these images.

Why take chances?

If it is bad TOSS IT!

Action 25: Your strap GOOD PILE should look like this. Straps in the good pile should have these things

- Spring in the cam buckle works well
- Webbing has a tapered and solid end that easily threads through the cam buckle
- No cuts or frays along webbing's sides

- Marking of strap's length (in rowing the two typical sizes are 9 or 12 feet). NOT a deal breaker but extremely helpful
- No knots. (They can weaken a strap's integrity by up to 40 percent)

Any sign of weakness means deposit that strap to the BAD pile.

Oh, and how many of your straps are probably weak or unusable? The following chart, based on years of observation, should give you some idea of annually how many of your straps are not in tip-top shape.

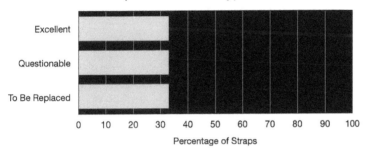

Straps Condition In Typical Boathouse

Percentage of Straps

There's no repairing bad boat straps

Take all the BAD straps and get rid of them. THEY ARE NOT SAFE. You can't fix them—so don't even go there. But you can find a home for the bad straps, such as recycling them for work away from the boat house or cut them up to make belts. But remember, they are now defective. Keep them out of your boat area!

This is why we did the sorting away from the boat house. As we mentioned before, here is a fact of boathouse life—if you bring even one strap from the BAD pile back to the boathouse sooner or later that strap will appear in your GOOD strap pile. Guaranteed. And trouble WILL happen.

Action 26: Your name on the straps. Now grab a Sharpie and write your name on every strap in the GOOD pile if it's not already on the strap. Then gather them up and transport them back to the boathouse.

A tapered edge with a smooth cut is critical. This one was cut with a hot knife with a temperature around 350 degrees.

Smart

The length
and name
on a strap
will save you
hassles.

Action 27: Boat strap storage. Store the GOOD straps inside, out of the sun and weather. Weather takes its toll on straps left in the sun or rain. Prolonged exposure to ultraviolet rays will cause the straps to degrade. Storing your straps properly, as with slings, will take some thought. And keep them dry.

Margot knew a collegiate coach who had a very impressive, efficient-looking rig on his trailer. He took a large wheel meant for holding garden hoses and attached it on the trailer's end. All straps went on there. At first glance it really looked slick.

BUT, weather takes its toll on straps left in the sun or rain. And, on this wheel, the innermost straps could stay wet. So it may have been convenient at races but it was ultimately not good for the straps.

Action 28: Replace your boat straps. If you are in the buying mood you'll have a lot of options and many (NOT all, but most) sellers will sell quality straps. But you need to make sure that what you are buying is exactly what you need. Buy boat straps for quality, not for price, or flash, or a fancy name woven in the strap. You want quality, and be prepared to spend anywhere from $5 to $10 per strap.

Nylon or polypropylene are the best materials to use since they are strong, dependable, and will not rot (degrade Yes, rot No). Of these, polypropylene is the most commonly used material in boat straps today. And remember to check the stitching, as Jim Pickens suggests.

Takeaway

No nicks, no cuts, no fraying edges. Straps not perfect? Toss 'em.

Rowing Racks: Where Your Rowing Equipment Spends 95% of Its Life

6

One day Mike was doing research and decided to tally up how rowing equipment spent its life. He came up with this interesting tidbit of information…rowing equipment spends 95% of its life in racks. Yep, that equipment you count on to glide you through the water is lounging away in a rowing rack almost its entire life. A life which looks something like this:

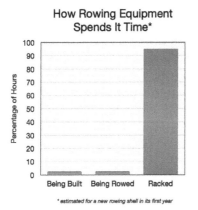

Let's make sure during that time your racks give the equipment the support and protection they deserve.

Rowing-shell racks

A rowing-shell storage rack (aka boat rack) is a structure designed and built to safely support a boat when it's not being rowed. A boat lays on it, in the seats-down position.

That position allows the boat to be supported by its superstructure and gunwales—the two strongest parts of the boat. This also keeps the relatively fragile area of the hull protected.

However, dent-time happens when boats are in racks and it's not uncommon for hulls to suffer a series of small insults while racked. The main culprits are the riggers from the boat in the rack above.

Oops

Gives new meaning to the term "rack and ruin"

If that boat on top is not moved carefully then the hull underneath can end up with scrapes, dents or punctures.

But more than dents can happen—we've actually seen the lower boat get knocked completely off the rack by the boat over it being carelessly handled!

In a moment we'll talk more about boat racks.

You can see a small amount of damage to the bottom hull from the rigger on the boat above.

Oar Racks

Like boats, oars need to be stored when not rowed. There are several different ways to store oars:

- *Vertically in racks:* with spoons-down (weight supported at collars)
- *Vertically in racks:* with spoons-up (weight supported by handle butt)
- *Horizontally:* laying on the side (weight supported by shaft)

Oars are awkward at best when off-the-water and, like boats, they can suffer damage in storage. But a quality rack can greatly reduce that.

What goes into a high quality rowing-shell rack or oar rack?

As you contemplate your boat and oars sitting patiently in their racks there are things to look for to make sure both pieces of equipment are safe and properly supported.

Vertical oar rack with oars blades-up,

For boat racks, look for:

- Racks designed and built to handle more weight than just the weight of the shell(s). You have to take into account the weight put on the racks from moving.

- Boat properly supported. Two supporting beams for a four or smaller boat, 3 beams for an eight.

- Space vertically between racks is large enough so boats can be moved in/out There should be several inches of clearance between hulls and riggers from the boat above/below.

- Beams are padded. This prevents damage to gunwales and reduces unwanted moving of boats.

- For boats stored outside, the boat should be able to be securely strapped (to reduce wind damage) and covered (to reduce UV damage)

Vertical oar rack with oars blades-down,

Douglas Lumsden, founder and owner of Space Saver Rowing Systems in Australia, told Mike this about quality boat racks:

A system that can be moved easily is important, because needs and designs in boat sheds will change. Also, a good quality set up should be built to last 30-40 years. And top notch padding is important—it will make a big difference to the boat's gunwales.

Horizontal oar rack.

For oar racks, look for:

- Racks designed to keep sets of oars together
- Oars which are stored vertically with blades-up, the handle butt should be on material (such as wood or padding) and not on floor
- Oars which are stored vertically with blades-down, the blade tip should elevated off the ground
- Oars which are stored horizontally, beams should be set a distance apart so oars lay balanced

Which type of oar storage option is best?

Lumsden noted that storing oars blades-down has several advantages, such as reducing the potential for hand infections (because water will drain away from the handles not toward the handles), easily locking oars into the racks, and saving space because the blades nest in nicely with each other. He also noted that:

> *Storing oars horizontally is often a great solution for boat sheds with low roofs.*

And his least favorite set up? Storing oars with blades-up.

What destroys a rowing-shell rack or an oar rack?

Racks tend to be some of the strongest structures in the boathouse (or should be). However, they do get damaged. What usually damages a rack and can make it unsafe is wear, neglect (no maintenance), and overloading. And since many racks are homemade it's not unusual to see fasteners loose or rusting, beams and supports becoming un-level, and padding torn or missing.

Over the years we've found on any given day about 1 in 10 racks need some attention, and about 1 in 50 are so substandard they endanger the boat and those around it. Let's see what condition your racks are in.

Action 29: Inspect your rowing racks. Inspecting your racks can be a challenge because often they will be occupied. So for your inspection either schedule it when equipment is being rowed, or in transit, or bring a work party with you to move things around.

The three main areas to check on your boat racks are:

1. The beams—are they all at the same height so the boat sits level? To do this use a tape measure and a level.

2. The fasteners—are they all tight? Use wrenches here, finger tight isn't tight enough.

The padding—is it securely attached to the beam and in good condition? If the padding is loose or separating it should be repaired or replaced.

You may find it helpful to mark each rack with either the boat that "lives there" or what size boat the rack can handle, with support and length.

Margot strongly suggests, Do NOT use PFDs for padding on your racks. They are needed elsewhere.

Action 30: Inspect your oar racks. Here are three questions to ask about your oar racks

1. Is the oar safely supported and won't fall out of the rack?

2. Are there areas where the oar could get damaged? For example, if stored blades-up could the oar's tip be damaged when the oar is inserted or removed from the rack?

3. Is the rack clearly labeled for the set of oars that is assigned to it?

Action 31: Repair your rowing racks. If you have manufactured rowing racks which are in need of repair, and it's beyond a simple correction by you (such as leveling a beam, tightening a fastener, or securing a pad) then contact the manufacturer for guidance. There's too much resting on the rack to not take that step (and while you are at it, ask if the rack is still under warranty).

If your homemade rowing racks are in need of repair then

you, or the handiest person in the boathouse, have the responsibility to get it fixed.

Action 32: Replacing your boat racks or oar racks. After many years of dealing with homemade shell racks in our boathouse Mike and staff had finally reached the end of their patience. They had spent hours-upon-hours leveling and padding beams and realized that their best efforts were not going to be good enough. So they took the plunge, signed a contract, and in a short time they had a brand new, sturdy, safe, and perfectly level rack system. It was so nice they actually had a party.

Remember

Inspect
Repair
Replace

If you are looking to make the leap to manufactured racks check out these dealers (and discuss installation with them):

- RowAmerica
- Space Saver Rowing Systems
- Swift Racing
- Wintech Racing

You'll find many different designs and options to help your equipment have a safe and supported rack life. And quality manufactured racks, such as those sold by Space Saver Rowing Systems, have a reputation of years of worry-free and low-maintenance use.

Takeaway

Keep racks safe, sturdy, and workable. The boats and oars are too important to do otherwise.

Boathouse Safety: Inside and Out   7

There are things in your boathouse that don't belong. Items that will cause you in the future to slap palm-on-forehead and say, "Ugh, why did I leave that there?"

Three times that has happened to Mike. Once he let an old strap sneak back in from the BAD PILE and it caused havoc. Another time a damaged sling ripped—almost destroying a perfectly decent boat. And another time you can imagine how high he jumped when he put on an old life jacket which had an inhabited mouse nest in it.

Let's reduce the chance that these mishaps and others will happen to you.

Smart!
If it stinks—
take it out!

11 things to remove from your boathouse

To start, when we say *remove* we mean one of two things:

Either: *Secure an item so only you or someone in-the-know can use it*

Or: *Move a thing from the boathouse so it is away from everyone*

Why do this? A few reasons, such as: reducing lost practice time, saving equipment from damage, avoiding race day hassles, and shrinking potential injuries. Think boathouse safety.

With those reasons in mind, here's a list of 11 things to remove immediately from your boathouse:

Action 33: Remove Bleach. Let us be clear…bleach CAN be a very helpful tool in the boathouse as we discussed in Chapters 1 & 4, but only in the right hands. It's easy to assume that using bleach is a no-brainer. No…it's not that simple. You must use bleach the right way because if it is used incorrectly bleach can and will cause significant damage.

Here's a few bleach thoughts from the experts:

- Bleach can expire. After a shelf life of six months, bleach starts to degrade. Even in its original bottle, bleach becomes 20 percent less effective as each year goes by.
- Bleach is more effective at killing germs when diluted than when used straight out of the bottle. Bleach mixed with water at a 1:9 ratio (i.e. 10 percent bleach) is potent for about a day (it is more unstable in its diluted form). For most uses, a ratio of nine parts water to one part bleach is recommended.
- Bleach is corrosive and can easily stain or destroy stainless steel.
- Bleach, when mixed with ammonia, can create toxic chloramine gases and an explosive called nitrogen trichloride.

So if you are going to keep bleach at the boathouse make sure only knowledgeable people use it. And yes, someone in a hurry to get on the water WILL pour straight bleach on something, which can be very dangerous.

Action 34: Remove Ammonia. We just discussed how dangerous ammonia can be around bleach. So with bleach probably in your boathouse remove any ammonia.

Action 35: Remove water fountain. With the struggles with viruses today every shared surface is a potential hazard. And a water fountain can be pretty disgusting. The bowl can gross out the best of us, with yuk in there because some people spit before drinking.

And want to be really grossed out: a 13-year-old conducted an experiment that tested his school's fountain water against the water from one of his school's toilets. After letting bacteria incubate, he found that not even the cleanest fountain was as clean as the toilet.

So eliminate water fountains. BUT people will need water, so rig up a system so they can get water safely and easily.

Action 36: Remove broken slings. There are two types of slings—those in excellent condition, and all-the-rest. You don't want to use the second type. As we noted in Chapter 5 you've got a lot riding in your slings—let's avoid a big let down. Take the marginal slings out of the boathouse until they get repaired or replaced.

Action 37: Remove substandard straps. Along that theme of bad things ending back up in the GOOD pile, boat straps will do the same. You think they're gone and...POOF...there they are—back on the trailer, with your primo-race-boat, once again, fearing for its life. Bottom line—you don't repair bad straps, you remove them.

Action 38: Remove critter homes. We already told you about Mike's mouse-in-the-life-jacket scare. To add to that we've experienced:

Busted?

Remove it!

- Bats in the workroom
- Rats in the rigger
- Blacksnakes in the eight
- Raccoons in the boat bay
- Alligators on the dock (yes…really)
- Geese on the dock (which probably attracted the alligators)
- Ducks in the launch
- Fire ants in the erg room
- Hornets in the megaphone

And the list goes on-and-on. We are an outdoor sport and work in open spaces and large areas. That means nature is always close at hand.

We recommend being as proactive as possible in reducing unwanted collisions with nature. Sometimes that means removing the critter (as humanly as possible, or just removing the potential attractions). For example, Mike had to call in

Our spaces make great homes for all sorts of animals. Try to remove/relocate them before the season gets going

removal experts for the bats (which closed down the workroom for weeks) but he avoided more raccoon visits by proactively removing all food from the boat bays. (And per the alligators…well…they just let them do their thing.)

Margot recently heard from some rowing pals that racoons had taken up residence in their boathouse. Of course, it being a Covid-aware time, lots of mask jokes followed.

Remember

Inspect
Repair
Replace

Action 39: Remove broken oars. We like to think of oars as indestructible. They are tough, but bad things do happen to good oars. And a broken oar being rowed can cause all sorts of issues.

Oars are too awkward to really make use of the two-pile system, so Mike suggests finding a place to put the oars that either need repair or are beyond repair—but NOT in the oar rack, even with a note on it. Some rower-in-a-hurry-with-a-coach-on-the-dock-screaming-to-get-a-move-on will be all too tempted to grab any oar handy—broken or not.

Action 40: Remove hammers. You might need a hammer… once-in-a-while. But most (*they* being 99% of the people using the boathouse) DON'T need a hammer. So hide yours. Tuck it away in a locked toolbox, or in your car. Out of sight, out of mind, OUT of dangerous hands!

Action 41: Remove locking pliers. Yes, yes, yes…locking pliers have their place in a toolbox to help remove broken screws or loosening frozen nuts—but only in trained hands. In other hands locking pliers can cause a lot of damage.

And then there was the novice rower who used locking pliers to grab the threads of rigger bolts to push them through the gunwale. He successfully, in 5 minutes, damaged the threads on 32 stainless metric bolts. Quite possibly a world record!

Action 42: Remove non-stainless fasteners. Let's just do this…gather up every non-stainless fastener in your boathouse

Why? Most non-stainless fasteners will rust which in our environment means a-lot-of-rust—and a rusting fastener can cause all sorts of issues. This is even more relevant if you're rowing in brackish/salt water. So remove all non-stainless from the boathouse.

And if you find yourself with secondary rowing projects in which you are going to use non-stainless, like building shelves, remove those fasteners from easy access because they WILL mysteriously appear mixed in with your rowing equipment, and we DON'T want that!

Action 43: Remove carbon fiber shreds. Carbon fiber and fiberglass are used throughout rowing. And although they are tough, they can break—leaving splinters. Those splinters can easily cut or get embedded in skin, causing pain and possible infection. Remove all shreds to a safe area and handle with care!

Takeaway

Inside and out, keep your eyes and ears open for items to remove, fix or install at your boat house. By taking these actions, you'll have a safer boathouse, safer dock, safer ramps and less to worry about.

Boathouse Checklist

- ❑ First Aid Kits
- ❑ Safety poster/reminders
- ❑ Emergency phone contact numbers
- ❑ Land line phone
- ❑ Log book (ELECTRONIC OR PAPER)
- ❑ Book to record all damages/ missing parts

Inside the Boathouse

Look around with a critical eye.

Is there any way someone could get hurt here?

Trip? Bang into something?

- Sharp edges on racks
- Slippery, oily floors
- Rags
- Riggers on the floor
- Boats in the aisles
- Misc. carts, wheels, pontoons, ergs? SPARE PARTS?
- Bottles, trash, broken glass
- Nails, screws, bolts on the floor.

Outside

The Docks and Ramps:

- Check for splintering wood or cracks.
- Broken wood pieces
- Anything slippery—
- Ice
- Bird droppings
- Moss
- Any debris:

- Trash
- Broken glass
- Fishing lures, lines and hooks

Fencing/barriers:

- NB: Your club can be liable if someone accesses your dock and comes to harm. Anyone. Not just members.
- Keep children, animals, people OFF your dock.

Make sure there are sturdy fences or barriers and signage about private property.

8

Rowing Life Jackets: A Critical Coaching Tool

The morning Mike should have drowned was a chilly Fall day. It was wicked early. He was in his launch. Checking buoys for a race. By himself. Flat water. The launch was wet with dew. He grabbed for a misplaced buoy. He reached. He slipped. He fell overboard. Cold water. Fully dressed. Pockets loaded with tools.

Be Smart!
Wear your PFD!!
Save your own life.

Mike didn't drown that morning because of a decision he made years before

Immediately after college Mike began work as a whitewater raft guide. It became second nature to wear life jackets (aka PFD—personal flotation device). Oftentimes he wore his 10 hours per day or more. Over the years he saw hundreds of rafters survive falling into raging rivers with frightening swims yet they were able to go home with a great story to share—thanks to their PFDs.

Because of those years guiding him, Mike made a decision to always wear his PFD when coaching. It saved his life that morning.

You make your own decision to wear a life jacket—or not

We don't share that story to talk or guilt you into wearing a PFD. But if you do wear one (fingers crossed you do) we want to share a few tips and actions about keeping PFDs ready to go for your season.

Action 44: Research the number, type and size of PFDs you MUST have. Depending on where you coach, regulations most likely require you to have PFDs in your launch.

For example, Mike coaches mostly in Maryland where he is required by the US Coast Guard (USCG) and Maryland's Department of Natural Resources to have one PFD for each person in the launch. And you may be required to carry PFDs for each rower you are coaching.

If Mike's launch is longer than 16 feet then he must also carry one throwable life jacket. You may have different requirements where you coach. So it's critical to research and know what you MUST carry.

For example, as just noted, Mike must carry life jackets in his launch—but there is also an EXACT type of life jacket he must carry. The throwable life jacket he mentioned has to be a Type IV but the others may be a different type.

What adds a layer of confusion to all of this is that in the US there are numerous types of jackets, ranging from Type 1 to Type V. Each is designed a bit differently. And to add to that, PFD types are a little different throughout most of the rest of the world, with life jackets regulated by the CE standard of Europe.

Accord to Marc Messing, at RowSafeUSA.org:

> *The principal difference…is that the US standard (for PFDs) is designed to provide flotation for a 330 lb person, while the CE standard is based on a 220 lb person. As a result…PFDs outside the US are generally lighter, less bulky, and often more comfortable.*

AND not only are there different TYPES but they also come in different SIZES, ranging from child to adult. So again, you need to research what you must have. You need to know the number of life jackets AND the exact type AND the sizes.

Action 45: Inspect your PFDs. It's one thing to have the correct number, type, and sizes of life jackets, but those PFDs need to be in good condition. Which means you will need to

Sizing!

If it doesn't fit, get one that does!

Your life depends on it.

Different PDFs for different people

inspect your life jackets. Mike inspect his at the beginning of each season and he uses the two-pile system. Specifically, he checks:

Life jacket with date, size and other information

- The fabric—for rips, deterioration, mold and/or mildew, and exposed foam

- The straps and buckles—are they adjustable? and do they function?

- The flotation material for water logging or crushed foam

Another item to check is the date. Some jackets will have dates of manufacturer stamped on the inside label. And if the date is not there, write the date when you got the jacket. When you do inspection, you will have an idea of how old and servicable it is.

Margot has noted that an inflatable, though costly, can be preferred by scullers. It works well and, as it is flatter, its small profile is less cumbersome.

Action 46: Extend your jacket's life. To keep your life jackets in good shape, and extend their lives, here are a few tips from the USCG:

- Don't kneel, sit on it, or stack items on it. A PFD will lose buoyancy if the foam in it is crushed

- Keep jackets dry, to ward off mold/mildew

- Stow jacket in well ventilated area
- Life jackets that aren't in good shape should be removed from the boathouse and disposed of promptly.

Action 47: Put your PDFs into action. When Mike coaches, he wears a Type III. It is comfortable and gives him plenty of flotation and visibility. He also requires anyone else in my launch to wear a Type III, and he carries a PFD for each rower he is coaching (in USRowing's Kippy Liddle Kits).

Get the best— *You are worth it!*

If you need to buy a PFD buy the best you can afford. Several companies make nice shortie-vests with reflective tape that come with pockets, and they're functional, comfortable, and very unobtrusive. Great for coaching and will give you funky tans, but will help keep you warm on cold days.

A good fit is critical for all rowing life jackets

A PFD on your body is a good thing. A PFD on your body that's been correctly adjusted is an even better thing. To get a good fit, buckle the fasteners and adjust the straps along the side of the PFD so that the fit is comfortable. Then grab the shoulder area on the jacket and pull up—the jacket shouldn't rise to cover your face. If it does, tighten the straps and test again. When it's correct, tuck in the side straps so they are out of the way. You should have each member of your team adjust and test their PFD in the same way.

(Mike has his coxswains wear PFDs in cold weather, both for flotation/safety and because it helps keep them warm.) BUT, see below:

Margot, working as dockmaster at many New England regattas, has repeatedly noticed that in cold weather a coxswain will layer up to stay warm, especially those from southern regions. A danger with that is that even with an approved flotation device on top, this may not be safe. If the boat flips (OK, not likely in an eight but, it can happen) the cox can really struggle with all those wet heavy layers on. And, could sink like a stone. Alternatively, a survival suit may be more suitable. And it's warm.

A caution, in a bow-loaded boat, the fit can be already tight for a coxswain. Add a survival suit, and the tight fit can be tricky for a coxswain to get out in case of emergency.

Takeaway

A PFD can save your life. And that of your rowers. Don't skimp here.

Transporting Rowing Equipment

9

First, Mike heard the sound. It was sickening. Then looking in his rear-view mirror he saw the shell as it came off the trailer, snapped in two, and crashed to the road. It'd been a heck-of-a-day and it just got worse. Much worse.

A long day just got even longer

He had left the boathouse at 4 a.m. and drove through pouring rain to the race course. They had battled rain and cold throughout the entire day. When they left the course to go home they were soaked. Frozen. And with marginal racing results to show for their efforts.

They had just moved 50 people hundreds of miles, got them on and off the water safely, and now just miles from home a rowing shell had died on his watch.

One battered-ego later he figured out what happened

After leaving the course that day Mike had been driving into a stiff-and-gusting crosswind. An older boat strap holding the bow of the boat couldn't take the stress and it snapped. The wind then shoved the bow off of his trailer. The stern strap, a new one, held tight. The sickening sound I heard was the boat breaking at the good strap. It was a mess but thankfully no one was hurt.

Transporting rowing equipment safely requires an over-investment. What we mean by that is to thoughtfully and methodically get the equipment ready for travel. It's a critical (and OFTEN overlooked...so often) component of safely transporting rowing equipment. Bluntly, the actions taken before....WELL before...you move the equipment—regardless of whether you are trailering or car-topping— will make all the difference.

We need to ask you three questions that might well keep what happened to Mike from happening to you.

Question #1:
Is your transporting vehicle ROAD-ready?

Before the season starts, check the critical parts of your shell trailer or car-top set up. Here are six different areas to dig into:

Action 47: Check the tires. Have the tread on your tires checked once a year by an expert. Never underestimate the importance of this action! Tires can and do wear out faster than expected, and you don't want to put anyone in danger (of course)...or miss a race because of a flat. And trailers often have older tires on them that could be marginal at best. (We have seen it recommended that tires over 5 years old should be replaced just due to the age of the materials.)

Read the recommended pressure on the sidewall of the trailer's tires. Then, pull out a tire gauge and check the tire pressure. If the pressure is low then fill the tires to the correct pressure—and yes, a difference of 5 psi does matter—just like .01 second can matter in a race. Don't forget to check the pressure on the spare tire as well. (You do have a spare, right?)

(And a hot tip...it is easier...by a factor of a hundred-fold... to find an air pump and put air in a rowing shell trailer when-the-trailer-is-empty. And while you are at it fill up the towing truck/car if that would make life easier too.) And, check tires for dry rot along the sidewalls of the tires, just in case.

Action 48: Check brakes and bearings. Brakes and bearings need checking and it is considered a normal maintenance action. More than one trailer driver cruising down the interstate has been passed by one of their own trailer-wheels that broke free because of a worn bearing.

And functioning brakes on a trailer can mean the difference between a sudden stop and a full-on collision.

A car-topped single doesn't add much weight to the car, but the added length and driving challenge puts more emphasis on the importance of stopping when you need to stop—in other words, check your brakes too.

Action 49: Check your visibility. Test every single light on the trailer, tow vehicle, and car. Yes, even the little ones that illuminate the license plate need to be checked—and working. (Mike got a $25 ticket once because ONE of the TWO license plate lights had burned out. You could still see the license plate at night but it wasn't "bright enough.")

Check!
Can you see? Everything tightly strapped down?

Notice that this trailer does NOT have its running lights working.

Check too that you can see around you. When too much gear is in the towing vehicle, you might have your vision obstructed. And a quick aside, don't have music at distraction-level. You need to be able to hear what is going on around you.

Red flags on all boats should be abundant and well affixed. Each shell should have one, whether on trailer or car top. The improvement in visibility of having lights and flags is huge. In many areas too, it is the law. Check your regulations, some require a large red flag. A thin strip of orange plastic is not sufficient.

Margot always does the "wiggle test" after every stop. She is looking (actually feeling) to see if the boat is still held tightly by its straps. Sometimes straps loosen after miles on the road. But, she has also encountered mischief. Someone had undone many straps while she dined at a rest area in the Mid-West. Had she not checked, she would have lost three very costly singles.

Action 50: Check trailer hitch/connector. How dirty…how greasy…how ABSOLUTELY critical a trailer hitch is! It's so worth your time to make sure that the socket, lever, and all connectors for your trailer are ready to go. And that you have chains which are attached securely. The night before the first trip is NOT the time to do that. Especially to make sure you know exactly where your trailer hitch is?

Careful out there!

Are you insured?

Action 51: Insurance. It's not exciting stuff, insurance. But you must have the right policies in place to protect your equipment, your program, and yourself. With that in mind, here are several questions to ask about your insurance

- Is the driver insured, regardless of whether he/she is a member of your organization?

- If the tow vehicle/trailer/or car is not owned by your organization, and there is an issue, whose insurance covers the vehicles? The equipment? Personnel?

- What areas of coverage are you lacking in, in terms of replacing damaged equipment, liability coverage, and deductible?

- What is the coverage if you are transporting someone else's equipment and it gets damaged?

Refer to Chapter 14 for more details on insurance.

Action 52: Plates and registration. More than one driver transporting rowing equipment has gotten a ticket for expired tags. Don't be that driver (your ego and your wallet WILL thank you).

Grab the registration card for shell truck, shell trailer or car, and check to make sure the registration and plates are current to-the-end-of-your-season. Then take pictures of them and put the hard copies in a place where you will have them handy WHEN (not IF) you need them. For more info on trailer regulations, read the excellent post *Shell Trailers and Their Regulation*, by the late Mark Schofer. You can find it on Row2k.com

Action 53: WARNING: Do NOT use a 15-passenger van for car-topping equipment. You are putting your life, and the life of anyone in the vehicle, and others on the road, in danger. And check with your insurance company about the number of people you can/should have in a 15-passenger van. At Mike's college only 9 people were allowed in a 15-passenger van when it was in motion.

Question #2. Is your vehicle EQUIPMENT-ready?

A *road*-ready vehicle is important. An *equipment*-ready vehicle with a trailer or car-top rack is critical. A few items to check:

Action 54: Check racks and pads. When transported, shells sit on racks or in car-top cradles. Chances are those racks, pads or the cradle have been baking-in-the-Sun and exposed to weather. That equipment is tough but ultraviolets are even tougher and the weather can do-a-number on those racks. Check yours for any corrosion or loose fasteners. Then turn your attention to the pads.

Pads not only protect the boat's gunwales but a good pad will help the boat sit securely on a rack (or in a cradle). Are your pads whole and securely attached to the racks? Make sure they are…it's CRITICAL.

Action 54: Space for other equipment. There's more to moving rowing equipment than motoring around just rowing shells. Riggers, slings, tools, tents, launches, outboard motors often travel with the boats …the list goes on and on. That stuff needs to go somewhere. Is your "somewhere" space ready? Sounds like a toss-away question, it is not!

Organize!

It's the fastest way to find what you need, when you need it.

For instance, the bottom deck of a trailer gets no respect. No love. No acknowledgment. Just abuse. Most are made of wood. And most will rot. Is yours in safe condition? Really? Will someone step on the deck and fall through? Will valuable hardware drop out of that hole in the deck and go missing?

What about that storage box you throw all your gear in… when's the last time you cleaned that out? And do you really have room for all your equipment in your car's trunk?

After the last trip across country, Margot took everything out

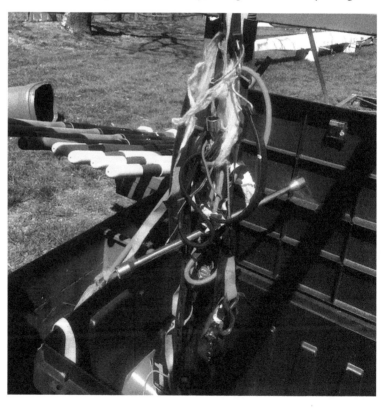

Check your boat box today so you don't have to deal with this mess on race day

of the trailer bed. Socks, socks and more socks, (mostly wet and white), shoes, hoodies, empty juice cartons. Hardware, tools. Straps. Despite her having done this exercise in California before departing for home, it befuddled and amazed her as to how and why this happened. Every time. So, sleeves rolled up, she dove in once again, purging and scrubbing.

Action 55: Boat straps. If you're unsure exactly how WE feel about boat straps, read Chapter 5.

Question #3: Is your DRIVER ROAD-ready?

Someone has got to drive the stuff…are they ready? Don't under-estimate (NEVER under-estimate) the power and impact of this. Your equipment and other vehicles and lives depend on it. See our chapter on readying your people, Chapter 16.

Mike was standing at a race one day, getting ready to go home when he overheard a conversation between two coaches. The head coach told his assistant (who self-professed OUT LOUD that he had never…EVER…driven a trailer) to go, hook up the truck to the trailer and then "drive that beast home." Then the head coach spun around and took off—leaving a bewildered assistant in his wake to fend for himself. Mike was dumbfounded…to put it mildly.

Drivers
A trained driver is a safe driver!

A fully loaded shell trailer is longer than most tractor trailers. It's a challenging monster to drive. A car-top with a double can have very dangerous and delicate overhang. Both vehicles take SKILL, PATIENCE, and a confident driver to navigate safely on streets and highways full of distracted drivers and numerous challenges. Add to that a layer of exhaustion from race day and a disaster can be just around the corner—literally.

Action 56: Train the drivers.

The time to train drivers is NOT on race day. As rowers we happily commit hours upon hours to learning the skills of our sport. Why not give the same attention to detail for driving a trailer? Use your "downtime" wisely and consider having your drivers (and potential drivers) take a workshop, and learn the skills needed. See the Chapter 16 for tips on that.

Practice is critical to safe driving. Get a mentor, hook up the truck and trailer (an empty trailer is best), and go drive. Go to a shopping mall (when the stores are closed and the lot empty) or a large open area and drive, drive, drive. Practice backing, practice parking, practice driving. When you feel comfortable with all that, crank it up a notch and do the same with a loaded trailer. Then, when ready for the highway, find an experienced trailer driver and head out for a road trip. Ride with that mentor and have them tell you what they are doing and why. "See that gas station ahead? Would I have room to clear the overhang? And could I pull out, or is it too constrained?"

Margot notes that your national governing body can be helpful. Check and see what resources they have for education. She helped produce a comprehensive video with USRowing, on Trailer Driving. We covered (and demonstrated) turning, avoiding poles and traffic light stands, overhang, loading, weight distribution, and dealing with other vehicles.

When she started driving herself, she had no idea how many dangers lurked: wind, rain, hydroplaning, other vehicles, downhills, fog, wind impact from large vehicles, fishtailing, backing up…

All of this might sound overwhelming, heck it IS overwhelming. But it's all critical. It's a big…*scratch* that… HUGE responsibility transporting rowing equipment. A few last suggestions, ones that we do, when getting things ready to roll:

Make a paper checklist, and check off items as we go.

Bring a coworker…many hands (and brains and ears and eyes) will make all these actions easier…and dare we add… more effective.

Bring a camera/phone and take pictures of questionable items, broken things, important numbers and pieces of paper.

Check out the route beforehand, be mindful of restricted roads and low overhangs. Some roads do NOT allow trailers.

Which side is your gas tank located on?

Margot always brings blocks. Before unloading or loading a trailer, place the blocks (or chocks, or heavy rocks, or cinderblocks) around the wheels. Stop the trailer from rolling, especially when it is unhitched.

Margot brings at least 6 bright orange cones with her on any trip, which will make vehicles in parking lots or on the street aware of your presence (especially buses and trucks). Station them all around your boats, and allow extra space.

This is also very useful to when parking, it keeps other vehicles from tucking in and parking under your boats, making pulling out VERY delicate.

Warning: These are not necessarily all of the steps you need to take for safe equipment transport. Check with your local experts for your individual needs and legal requirements for safe and legal transport.

Takeaway

Trailer-driving can be one of the most under-pressure, stressful aspects of our sport. Impatient rowers, impending weather, deadlines, all take their toll. Prepare now, in the calm time. Create your checklists and use them. And stay in charge of the process.

PS: The most common causes of accidents involving crew trailers:

1. Poor driving skills

2. Lack of good visibility

3. Improper tying of shells.

4. Weather: fog, ice, wind

5. Overtired driver

So it's critical that you pay attention. Want to know more about safe trailer driving? See *Checklist for Safe Trailer Driving and Loading* in the Appendix.

Trailer Checklist

- ❏ The shells/Boats
- ❏ Oars
- ❏ Riggers
  - ❏ Tie them together, for each boat.
  - ❏ Mark them to be sure they are from the correct boat and also P/S
    - ◆ Do not use duct tape to do so, it can be gummy.
    - ◆ Masking tape or Sharpies work. Or paper tape.
- ❏ Seats from boats and extras
- ❏ Tool Kit (see Appendix # 5)
- ❏ Extra Straps
- ❏ Bungees (and small ones if you bungee the seats in on the boat)
- ❏ Extra shoes

Red Flags

Check your regulations. There may be specifications about size and color. A small orange piece of plastic is not necessarily legal.

- ❏ Owner's paperwork
- ❏ Auto and Trailer registration
- ❏ Extra chain
- ❏ Rope
- ❏ List of all boats you are carrying.

If not a club boat, list owner, any existing damage, contact information and insurance. (Check and list all existing damage, so you are not held responsible later. Take photos.)

Rowing Spare Parts: Little Pieces— Big Advantage

10

It was late in the morning at a regatta and Mike had just finished checking the rigging on an eight—putting the last tweaks on it for the qualifying heat—when a fellow coach ran up, coming to a screeching halt.

Between gasps for air he managed to get out,

> *"Yo...Vespoli rigger...two top bolts...fell off in the trailer...can't find them...racing in 60 minutes!"*

Mike had a few extra bolts—gave him two (three actually)...and off he ran. Later that day the Coach swung by, this time at a more leisurely pace.

> *"You saved me. We looked and looked but couldn't find those dang bolts. I got yours back just in time. We launched but arrived at the line late and got a false start. The stress flustered the kids to no end and about killed me. We barely made it...and don't tell the kids this but I ended up puking in the bushes afterwards."*

The right spare part at the right time can save the day!

The super-power of rowing spare parts

Spare parts, those bits and pieces standing by to replace something missing, something broken, or something faulty, can be invaluable. A true gem of the tool box. But unfortunately too many (way TOO many) coaches see rowing spare parts as a luxury (they are NOT). They are, and always have been—a necessity.

Why Spare Parts?

As the boatman for the US national team, nightmares about spare parts would wake Mike up at 2:37 a.m. all the time. Something would break at the worst possible moment and there he'd be…wishing he had a spare part with none to be found…and Olympic athletes getting ready to toss him off a cliff.

Because of that he became, and still is, obsessive about spare parts for his rowing equipment (and just about everything in his life). Spare parts can save the day and they can do more too. A Stash of Spare Parts can and will:

- Maximize practice time
- Turn issues into opportunities
- Reduce friction
- Reduce cannibalization (taking a good part currently in use to replace a part somewhere else)
- Save valuable (almost priceless) water time
- Reflect positively on the holder
- Is a competitive advantage
- Saves $$$
- Reduce the time you spend puking in the bushes

It comes down to this, if YOU want to be effective (as a rower/coach/coxswain) you will have spare parts. Those who have spare parts look wise, are cool, and can be wickedly helpful. Those who don't have rowing spare parts will always be dependent on, AND indebted to, those of us who do have them.

Margot was helping an eight launch at the Head of the Charles Regatta and their steering line cable broke. The coach couldn't fix it, everyone panicked, and then a passing bicyclist/rower chimed in, "I bet a bike store would have what you need."

She drove the coach to the nearest bike store, (it being Cambridge, they were plentiful) he got the cable, did a seat-of-the-pants repair, and off they went. Not necessarily a spare part he would have brought, but… we had the wits to improvise.

Can you carry everything you might possibly need? Nope. But try.

Working with Rowing Spare Parts

How many and what type of spare parts do you need? We have a mental mandate when it comes to spare parts: We look around for things which could malfunction (break, go missing, etc.) and could bring whatever we're doing to a screeching-halt. That's exactly what we want a spare part for—to avoid that. In other words, Small Piece >>> Big Impact.

You don't have to scratch your head too hard to imagine what that could be for a rowing practice:

- rigger top bolt/nut
- seat wheel
- rigger bolt
- oarlock

When a part like one of those goes bad it stops a practice cold. So those spare parts are always with me.

What parts to stash?

If you're looking for recommendations of parts to have, the list below has several. It is by NO means an exhaustive list but we dare to include it here with the thought that it might get you thinking about what YOU should have:

- oars (check for their being the correct oars and the right sides P/S
- rigger (including assorted parts and frame)
- seats (or at least wheel(s) or undercarriage)
- bow ball and tape to fix it if necessary
- electronics and chargers
- boat straps
- fin
- microphone
- assorted stainless nuts and bolts
- oarlocks
- oarlock pins

- rudder and cable
- Bow numbers
- slings
- spare rigger(s) for each shell
- extra set of vehicle keys
- extra heel ties (or zip ties, shoelaces)
- assorted tapes; for hands, equipment, breaks.

The container for your spare parts does not have to be fancy. Whatever helps you find what you need, fast. works works!

Two stashes that we don't usually think of as spare parts, but need consideration are first aid kits and tool boxes. It's important what is in them and where they are located. See the Appendices lists of recommended items.

Three Stashes of Spare Parts

Try having three stashes of spare parts, each to use at a specific time and place. Build out one or all for your own rowing workflow:

Action 57: Build your Practice Stash. Those small items mentioned above, plus anything else a specific boat, or workout, will rely on (for example, batteries for indoor rower workouts). Anything that wears out or breaks frequently is a prime contender for the Practice Stash box.

Action 58: Build your Race Stash. The Practice Stash PLUS bigger items, such as a spare oar, bow numbers, entire seats, rigger stays, foot stretchers…anything and everything that you could/would/should need. Sometimes it looks like you will have brought the entire boathouse. Come to think of it… you might just do that.

Brent Bode, Traveling Boatman at Community Rowing, Inc. and instructor for the Institute for Rowing Leadership spent time in the trenches (and pits) of Indy race cars. A teammate used to tell him this about spare parts:

"If we don't pack it in the trailer we are sure to need it on race weekend. So pack everything!"

Wise advice, and for tools too!

Action 59: Build your Boathouse Stash. Practices and Race Stashes above, along with any other parts that need replacing frequently. For instance, Mike would have a stash of replacement seat tracks, quick release shoes, fins and rudders—and more, much more.

Where to get your spare parts

Action 60: Find your spare parts supplier. Often…but not always…you can get spare parts from the manufacturer. In fact, many boat builders will include spare parts kits with purchases or have them ready to buy separately.

However, in some countries there is NO LEGAL OBLIGATION FOR A MANUFACTURER TO HAVE AND KEEP SPARE PARTS. So the day may come (or it's already arrived) where you can't get a spare/replacement part for an older piece or speciality equipment. If that's your situation you may need to turn to other sources. Here are a few recommendations:

- Hardware store: for fasteners and non-rowing specific items
- Online store: several companies, such as Adirondack Rowing carry spare parts for a wide range of equipment
- Cannibalization: be careful about robbing Peter to pay Paul. Meaning DO NOT take things currently in use as a spare part, because that *thing* seldom, if ever, gets put back. However, that shell that hasn't been rowed in years (and the future doesn't look very promising for it either) could be a good source of spare parts.
- Friends/family/fellow coaches: could be helpful in a pinch. Don't forget quick and prompt repayment. Too many relationships have soured when repayment is delayed or never happens. DO NOT BE THAT COACH.

Action 61: Where should your spare parts stash live? Tom Peters is known to say (quite often) "Excellence is the next

5 minutes." A version as it relates to the topic at hand is: *Excellence is having spare parts exactly when and where you need them.* You don't want to have to run two miles back to a trailer for a spare part while your crew waits on the dock to launch. All this might sound like an oversimplification but it's not. It's reality.

The other part of this reality is that what works for us, in reference to what we put our spare parts in and where we keep them may not work for you. Our situations are different enough to require different solutions.

We suggest finding a container, a home, a nest, a whatever-you-want-to-call-it, and put your spare parts in it. As long as it is where you need it, when you need it—you've got a winner.

The container for your spare parts does not have to be fancy. Whatever helps you find what you need, fast.

Oh, and Bode's Top 5 Spare Parts are:

1. Oarlock Spacers
2. Skegs / Fins for all boat types and sizes (includes rudders for coxed boats)
3. Heel Ties
4. Bow Balls
5. Lane Numbers (for spring racing season)

Takeaway

Bits and bobs are small treasures. Be the one with the right top nuts, the right parts, and your stress will disappear.

Rowing Electronics: Your Assistant Not Your Boss

11

Mike had everything in his launch. Stroke-watch, GPS, cell phone, walkie talkie, power megaphone. He was all set for a successful practice. Instead, practice was terrible and here's why:

- The batteries in his stroke watch died
- He had GPS connection issues
- His cell phone rang numerous times, and he almost dropped (threw) it overboard
- The walkie talkie picked up a local trucking company conversations
- And his megaphone produced feedback that would have rivaled any rock guitarist

So why was practice so bad? Those issues themselves weren't what made the practice terrible. What did was his distraction. He became laser-focused on the electronics and before he knew it time had run out and he was on the return dock. No improvement to show and frustration on everyone's face.

Water time is limited—often a luxury, and distraction is the breeding ground of a substandard practice.

Distraction is a major down-side of electronics

But of course, there's an upside to using rowing electronics—and there better be for the investment you make. Rowing electronics are tools. When used effectively they can help improve rowing performance and safety. To get those benefits—the improvement in performance and safety—you must be methodical. Take actions to help make that happen. You don't need many actions—six actually—and we're going to make recommendations on those actions in a moment.

However, before we dive in we want to emphasize that all six can happen at any time, but BEFORE your season gets rolling along at full speed is probably the best time.

6 Actions For Maximizing Your Rowing Electronics Investment

None of the following six actions are tricky. None require coding nor magic abilities. But they will take time (maybe an hour per type of electronics) and effort. Here we go:

Action 62: Have a powerfully good reason why you use it. Why are you using that piece of rowing electronics? Because there is a benefit, right? But is the benefit worth it?

A coach called us a while ago. He was having trouble setting up his Peach system (an instrumentation system used to measure speed, catch angles, and power application). We asked him why he was using the system and we remember to-this-day his answer:

> *"Because I'm afraid other coaches will get it, and I don't want to be left out."*

FOMO (fear of missing out) is not a good reason to be using a piece of rowing electronics. You have to be careful about getting sucked into the rowing electronics arms race. From a simple stopwatch to a rowing app to the most sophisticated

Helpful or Harmful.

motion-analysis-program, the electronics should help you reach your goal. If they don't then why do you have them? Ask yourself, "Do I really need this item in my Rowing Universe (right now)?" If the answer is NOT a resounding, "Heck Yeah!" then don't buy it, or stop using it until it can help you. In other words—there MUST be a powerfully good reason you are using it.

Action 63: Learn how to use your electronics. Megaphone, speed meter, stopwatch, or other electronic gizmo...do you know how to use it? Most people just wing it and jump right in—they give it a go often without looking at the directions. To maximize your investment, really learn how to use the electronics. Read the instructions. Absorb a manual. Watch a tutorial. Talk to a user.

Years ago, Mike was only using 1/2 the potential of his Speed-Coach XLs. Then at a conference he asked for (and got) a hands-on session from an N-K employee. After that he became much more effective with the XL—learning how to use it in such a way so as not to overwhelm and distract himself and the rowers while getting valuable information. That conversation was critical.

What about you? How can you get better at using an electronic tool you have?

Action 64: Test it. Once you have an understanding of how the electronic is supposed to work then it is time to test it! Take your power megaphone and go yell in the woods—wake up some chipmunks. Take your speed system for a shake-down row. Use that stroke watch to measure everything. Try it. Test it. Get comfortable with it before you bring it full scale into your rowing workflow.

This is especially important if you depend on your electronics for safety. One year a regatta was having problems with boats capsizing and rescue efforts were a bit of a mess. Why? The volunteers and the emergency responders were on different radio systems and could not communicate effectively.

Action 65: Use it and evaluate it. Now that you:

- Know WHY you are using it
- Know HOW to use it
- Have TESTED it

…start using it. Welcome the tool into your rowing schedule and weave it into your workflow. Then after a period of time has passed reflect back on the reason why you have the electronics in the first place and evaluate if the tool is getting you closer to your goal. It's a simple process and we've used the following three statements to help us evaluate if an electronic tool is beneficial or not:

1. This tool is HELPING me in pursuit of a goal

2. I AM NOT SURE if this tool is helpful

3. This tool is HINDERING me in pursuit of my goal

Review those statements often and if a trend appears then act on it. For instance, Mike once made a multi-item purchase of one piece of electronics because it was apparent that it was quite helpful during testing, while at the same time he was returning another piece because it was constantly a distraction and hindering his coaching.

Action 66: Fix-it. Rowing electronics usually work well but then…something breaks or gets weird. Here's the tricky part—most broken rowing equipment follows an adjust/repair/replace Fix-It model. For example, if a seat is not working correctly:

1. You try to ADJUST it. If that doesn't work,

2. You try to REPAIR it. If that doesn't work,

3. You REPLACE it.

But with broken rowing electronics the Fix-It model is different. If it's not working correctly:

1. You try to ADJUST it. If that doesn't work,

2. You send it off for repair and in the meantime replace it or go without

The internal repair-step has almost completely disappeared

in most boatsheds and boathouses around the world. For the most part rowing electronics are no longer consumer repairable.

Action 67: Store it. When storing electronics you NEED to know what the manufacturer recommends because you can do damage if you don't follow their suggestions.

Typically you store rowing electronics in a cool dry place. But what do you do about the battery? Leave it in/take it out? Store it charged or uncharged? Check with the manufacturer for their most current advice (yes, of course, pun intended).

And remember where you stored your electronics because they can easily get misplaced. Also keep other stuff from being stacked on top of your electronics. We can't tell you how many times we've lost a stroke-watch or microphone only to find it buried beneath a pile of other stuff somebody stacked on it.

Somewhere under this pile is probably that stroke-watch or microphone I've been looking for

Takeaway

When you welcome a piece of rowing electronics into your rowing workflow, it is a tool. It is there to help you, don't let it be a distraction.

12

Coaching Launch Maintenance: Set Up Your Coaching Launch for Success

You just launched for practice. On your clipboard is the perfect practice plan. Healthy lineups sit in a fleet of boats before you. Gorgeous rowing weather is all around. Then...your engine stops. It won't start.

You try and try to get the motor going. You curse. You pray. But it refuses to start. Now what? You grab your paddle and inch your way back to the dock, creeping along as your rowers waste time—valuable time.

Then a few days later you're having a wonderful practice and things are splendid. Suddenly you notice a police boat behind you. The officer is demanding that you stop.

A clean, safe and mechanically ready to go coaching launch helps get practices off to a good start

"Where is your registration?" he asks. "Your life jackets, your sound device?"

As he writes you a ticket your rowers sit...muttering...missing yet another chance to get better.

No one wants to lose practice opportunities

It amazes us how many coaches don't bother to make sure their coaching launch is ready for success until there's an issue. THEN the launch gets the attention it deserves but usually way too late.

Do yourself a Big. Fat. Favor.

Get your launch ready for success early. Here's exactly what we mean by SUCCESS: invest time, effort, money so you have a coaching launch that is:

1. Mechanically fit

2. Meets regulations

3. Is safe and has the appropriate safety equipment

Fits your coaching style

You need all of those. Not just one. You need ALL! Point blank—this is not just about having a productive practice. This is about reducing injuries. Avoiding headaches. Saving money. Being a positive example. And not destroying your back from tugging hundreds-of-times on the pull-cord of a motor that has absolutely no intention of starting.

See Appendix 3 for a recommended operational checklist for the coaching launch.

What we mean by success

To help you get there we're going to recommend 12 critical Actions for you to take. Do each—they are based on things we learned. They are best to do before the season starts but if you are already rowing then do them when the opportunity arises. Coaching launch maintenance is important (scratch that…CRITICAL). Let's get you to success.

Get your coaching launch mechanically ready

A lot goes into having a coaching launch that runs well… day…after day…after day. Like a car, a coaching launch needs regular preventative maintenance. Too often it doesn't happen.

Sure, good excuses abound—but your launch doesn't care about your excuses. Instead, your coaching launch DE-MANDS regular and methodical attention. And it will let you know if it is not getting it. With that point hopefully

This is not what you want to have to deal with during a practice

made here are three actions to focus on:

Action 68: Outboard motor. Get the motor serviced. The manufacturer prescribes how often maintenance should happen. Follow that schedule closely. Call your local outboard motor shop. Trailer the launch and make a delivery. Or if that won't work have them come to you.

Ask the mechanic to tank-test the motor, tune it up, and give it a prop check. And if your motor uses propeller shear pins ask if they should be replaced, or at least pick up a few spare ones to put in your tool box (see the Appendices for a recommended basic tool box).

Action 69: Gas tank & hose. Have the mechanic test your gas hose and tank(s). Those items wear and break so you need to make sure they work and are clean on the inside. Don't wait for your first practice to do this.

When the launch is ready, get a full supply of the oil that you'll need for your rowing season. If you mix gas and oil, you'll probably need 50:1. If you don't mix, get the amount of oil you need. Stash the oil safely—motor oil has a way of sneaking off.

Action 70: Check your launch's hull. What's the condition of your hull (inside and out)? Does your launch need:

- Bottom paint?
- A seat repaired?
- Holes patched?
- Interior cleaned?

Those repairs can take longer than you think so it's best to do them now—in the middle of season there won't be time.

Those three actions (outboard motor serviced, tank & hose checked, and keeping your hull in good shape) will go a long way to keeping your launch ready and willing when you need it.

Check your coaching launch registration & insurance

There are three actions to focus on:

Action 71: Registration. On most public waterways a motorized boat will need to be registered. It's the operator's duty to make sure the registration is updated and properly displayed. If you are unsure what this entails contact your local authorities since the requirements can vary by location.

Keep any boat registration cards handy and in an easily accessible place. A copy on your phone could come in handy. Mike has been pulled over twice on the water—checking the bow numbers on his launch and his registration. In both instances everything was up-to-date and that saved him tickets and fines.

Action 72: Insurance. Is your launch insured? Many aren't but it might be worth considering if yours isn't. Check Chapter 14 for more details on insurance.

A safe coaching launch

A launch and safety go hand-in-hand. Here are four actions to take:

Action 73: Paddle. When your launch stops running—as it invariably will do despite your best efforts—how will you get to safety? You'll use your paddle, right? Where exactly is that paddle?

We can't tell you how often coaches say, "Oh yeah, there's a paddle in the launch," when that paddle is NOT in their launch but instead it is stashed somewhere in the boathouse in a pile of junk or in the trunk of their car. Before you reach for your paddle in a time of need, locate it. Write your name on it. And then stick the paddle in the launch. And every time before you shove away from the dock make sure that paddle is in the launch with you.

Action 74: Launch lights. Let's talk about being in the dark, specifically rowing in the dark.

Several times per year (or more often than that) most of us find ourselves rowing in low- or no-light. Or in fog. Times when we need to have lights for the launch and shells. We've seen too many coaches brush off the importance of lights, or just wing it…like using their cell phone flashlight for a launch and four eights. This is a crucial safety issue.

If you row in low-light times, or in fog, you must have lights. And lights that meet regulations. So, first of all, find out what the regulations are for where you row. Then get the launch lights you need. Then, since you are on a roll get lights for each shell. Several manufacturers make reliable and durable lights. Search them out and get what you need.

Action 75: PFDs. We talked about PFDs in Chapter 9 but let us reiterate this key point now—make sure you know the requirements for PFDs, meet them, and stay compliant. We're of one mind about having and wearing life jackets. You do what YOU must but we can share that we know of three coaching-friends who would have probably drowned had they not been wearing their life jackets. We're very grateful they were.

Action 76: Communications. When you are miles away from home on an isolated stretch of water how are you going to reach out when something goes wrong (and something will go wrong)? Your communication device (phone or radio, or better yet...BOTH) needs to be in good working order and fully charged before each time on the water.

And don't forget a sound generating device. Bring a whistle...the batteries never run down! Or for an isolated stretch of water, an air horn.

Set up your coaching launch to fit your coaching style

Action 77: Your coaching style. You have a physical style of coaching you are comfortable with. Are you the coach who must drive the launch, coach, run the stopwatch and do everything under the Sun? Or do you prefer to just coach and have someone do the driving and other things? Do you prefer coaching standing up, or sitting? Coaching from one side only, or all over the place?

Mike is most coaching comfortable and at his best/safest not driving but sitting in the front of the launch, coaching the boats from all sides. If your assistant and you know your preferences then set up your launch for you. Be comfortable, be safe and you'll coach your best.

Bonus Actions:

And here are two bonus actions to consider:

Action 78: Lock it up. You know what sucks...getting ready for an early morning practice, walking down to the dock to put things in your launch, and discovering your launch is missing. Like *gone*. Ugh!

If you keep your motor attached to the launch, is it securely attached? Locked on so only the right person at the right time can remove it. Small outboards hanging off a launch transom parked off a remote dock are prime targets for thieves. And is the launch secured? And the gas tanks and hoses? A word

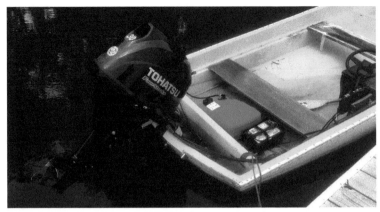

Don't underestimate the amount of water a good rain storm can deposit in a coaching launch.

to the wise from someone who has had two launches stolen from him—secure it all.

Action 79: A dry launch. Launches are great at collecting rainwater. Unless you have set up an automatic bilge pump, or you have a self-bailing launch, someone is going to be doing some bailing. Get it done before practice starts. Coaching WHILE bailing is no fun.

Critical, train your launch drivers. Make sure they know how to drive, yes, but also, how to rescue, how to dock, and how to be smart about conditions. See also checklists for what they need to have on board. Some jurisdictions may require a Boater Safety License, or training. See Chapter 16 page 94, on training your people.

Takeaway

Have what you need right at hand. Never have to regret that the critical life-saving device or rigging tool is back at the boathouse. Use the checklist to remind yourself what is important, no… critical.

Checklist

In the US, the national governing body USRowing sells the Kippy Liddle kit, which contains:

- ☐ Telescoping 24" paddle
- ☐ Rescue Throw
- ☐ Waterproof High Intensity Flashlight
- ☐ Air Horn
- ☐ Waterproof First Aid Kit
- ☐ Emergency Blankets
- ☐ Adult USCG-Approved PFDs

Those are excellent safety tools to have with you.

Some other items to consider equipping a launch with are:

- ☐ an anchor
- ☐ bailers
- ☐ additional paddles
- ☐ rope
- ☐ fire extinguishers
- ☐ extra line
- ☐ flare kit

Depending on the size of your launch some of those items may actually be required.

On the Launch:

Does the launch have enough life jackets for every rower, coxswain and coach?

- ☐ Keep launch lights working
- ☐ Carry VHF, FM marine radio or cell phone for communication and possible rescue. George Kirschbaum adds, Some may use the marine VHF radio for intra-squad or across squads to communicate, especially in an emergency. And to call for Marine Police assistance.

❑ Everyone in the launch should wear a life jacket, especially the coach.

First aid kit

Tools

❑ Basic tool kit (see appendix #5.)

❑ Cell phone

❑ Pen and paper

❑ Waterproof container for tape measure, pen and paper, etc.) spare oarlocks, oar buttons and seats

❑ Rigger top bolts or nuts

Check:

❑ Is your gas tank full?

❑ Has there been any damage since your last practice?

❑ Is the plug in and secure?

❑ Do all lights work?

❑ Is the bilge pumped out if necessary?

❑ Do you have at LEAST the required number of PFDs?

❑ Do you have communication to shore?

❑ Is the prop clean or is it fouled by your tether line or debris?

❑ Do you have at least one paddle?

❑ Are you wearing your PFD?

❑ Is the motor pumping water?

❑ Do you have:

    ❑ An anchor?

    ❑ A non verbal communication device?

    ❑ First aid kit?

    ❑ An on-the-water tool kit?

    ❑ Rower-specific health equipment? (such as inhaler, Epi-pen, etc.?

Rowing Shell Preparation: Get Your Shell(s) Ready to Row

13

It was a blazing-hot Florida day. Mike was busy, elbow-deep in boat work. He had to leave a boat outside in slings—in the sun. That boat, named after the President of his University, "Jerome P. Keuper" was a single-skin fiberglass eight. It was old but still in decent shape.

Around mid-day, with the sun at full strength, the fiberglass of the Keuper's hull gave way. The heat and years of sunlight caused the fiberglass in the boat to give up its strength and turn to mush. The part of the shell sitting on the slings caved in and the boat crashed to the ground. The Keuper was a total loss. The best part of his day was informing his boss and the President of the school that he'd destroyed his boat.

Since then Mike has always visualized a shell as a living thing with the thought that if he cared for it, fed it, loved it, it would take care of him. Sure…it's hippie-thinking (but that's Mike), but he's worked with hundreds and hundreds of shells over the years and that thinking has always served him well.

How do you get your rowing shell ready to row?

Imagine you've been on vacation for an extended period… when it's finally time to go back to work it is a significant shift. You've got to get ready for a new routine. New work-flows. New actions. The same for a shell.

As Dickie Pereli, owner of Inriver Tank and Boat told us:

> *"The time and effort you put into caring for your shell*
> *BEFORE the season is like taking care of your car*
> *before a long trip. No one wants to be stranded on the*

side of the road, missing out on the vacation you've planned for years. The same with rowing—investing now into shell maintenance will help you get where you want to go."

A shell that has been dormant for a few weeks (or longer) needs to be prepared to get back to work. And to help you get yours ready there are actions you will need to take. A few side-benefits of these actions are:

- Increasing the life of the shell
- Reducing injuries
- Saving money
- Having more productive practices
- Missing less water time

Five specific zones to help you fine tune your rowing shell preparation

To make things easier divide your shell into five Zones. Put your focus on each Zone and try to work only in that Zone until it's done. Then you can move onto the next Zone. This will help you focus and conserve time and resources. Each Zone has several actions to take.

To be clear, these actions are NOT about making rigging adjustments and fine tuning for speed. That comes later. These actions ARE about getting the equipment READY for those adjustments and preventive maintenance. The work BEFORE the work, if you will. The assignments before the exam. Off we go to rowing shell greatness:

Zone 1: The Hull (inside & outside)

Of all the equipment we have in rowing there's one piece you cannot ignore—the shell's hull. It's big. It's important. And it needs love and attention. And it will eventually get all it needs…when it leaks, or breaks. But why wait until something bad like that occurs? Head those issues off-at-the-pass.

Action 80: Clean the hull. Start by cleaning the outside of the hull. Cleaning it by hand can give you a feel for dings, dents

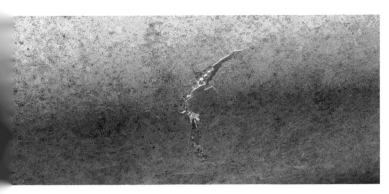

Dirt and cracks like on this hull will not only slow the boat down but can cause injury. Look carefully.

and worse. We typically wash a hull with dish soap and water unless it needs to keep dry for a repair. In that case, just wipe the dust and dirt away with a dry cloth. (It is amazing how dusty a shell gets sitting in the racks.)

Action 81: Fix dents and holes. When cleaning, did you find dings/dents/holes? This is the best time to fix them. Delaying SMALL repairs often means they won't get done until they turn into BIG repairs.

Monocoque design, notice platform that extends from gunwale-to-gunwale, and access holes (image from Wikipedia)

Action 82: Check and repair any superstructure issues. Turn the boat seats-up and check the insides. There you will find the superstructure, which gives the boat its strength and rigidity.

The superstructure is usually one of two different types, depending on the manufacturer. For example, some shells are made with supporting braces throughout the boat, while others may use a horizontal deck called a monocoque-decking system.

Regardless of the method used the superstructure takes a lot of wear and tear. In fact, every time a stroke is taken there are forces that work against the structure. Therefore it's critical that the boat's structure is maintained. If it isn't then the boat will lose its rigidity and become inefficient. So, look for structural parts that are broken or loose. Inspect the cross members for cracks and break, and places where the fiberglass has rough edges and could injure rowers. For small issues, make a note to keep a watchful eye on them, and for bigger concerns get it repaired—pronto.

Action 83: Bowball and bow number holder. This is a perfect time to make sure the bowball is safe (meaning it is in good shape and attached securely) and the clip for the bow number is also securely attached. More than one rower has missed a race due to no bow ball, and more than one race result has been contested after the fact due to a bow number that didn't make it to the finish line. Why? Safety, safety, safety. A bowball protects others should a collision occur. Heel ties let you get out of the boat quickly.

Margot has been dockmaster for many years. She knows it is always painful to disqualify a boat before they even launch. If they have NO Bow Ball, or it is barely being held by strands of ancient duct tape, they cannot launch at a registered regatta.

She felt awful as she reduced a high school boat of intense young rowers at the Head of the Charles Regatta to tears. No bow ball, and only a few threadbare heel ties. They had traveled from Texas to compete, but their coach had not come prepared. Margot sent them back to remedy the situation, with hopes that they could borrow what they needed and meet their launch time.

Zone 2: The Seats

Seats are critical for function AND for comfort. Don't cut corners with seats. Nothing will distract a rower quicker than a squealing seat (like fingernails being dragged down a blackboard) or an uncomfortable seat-top.

Action 84: Clean and inspect. Remove each seat and give each a cleaning. Clean around the axles and wheels. Then inspect the wheels. Are they in good shape? Like the tires on your car, seat wheels wear and need replacing.

If yours show signs of wear, such as cracks, breaks or reduced size, replace with new ones. And check to see if the wheels are securely attached (sometimes the fasteners on the end of the axle will come loose). Then make sure that the right seat is returned to the right place (boat and position). Double check for magnets for electronic sensors.

Action 85: Condition of seat top. This is a critical comfort area for every rower. The top needs to be clean, smooth and without issue. If it is not in a condition which YOU would want to sit on for hours at a time then fix or replace. Wooden seats can develop cracks and splinters.

Action 86: Condition of tracks. Now turn your attention to the tracks. Good shape? Or pitted, aged, bumpy? Tracks, like seat wheels, wear and need replacement, and new tracks often improve the feeling of rowing. We've found it best to replace both tracks at a position at the same time, but if your budget is tight replacing one at a time can work.

Pitting and bumps on slide

These are indications it is time to look at replacing the tracks. If you do replace one consider doing both port and starboard together.

Zone 3: The Foot Stretchers

The foot stretchers are critical to function and comfort and each of the following actions apply to both standard foot stretchers or quick-release foot stretchers.

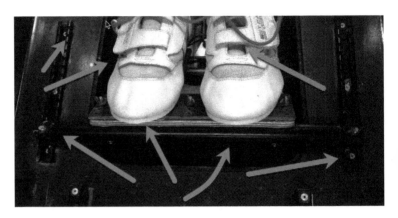

Prime areas to check on foot stretchers

Action 87: Correct sizes. Are the sizes of the shoes correct (or even in the ballpark) for the rowers? The closer the size to the rower's actual foot size the better the rowing. And YES I know (all too well)...many of you are in situations where different people will be cycling through the seats, and that makes sneaker sizing a crazy time. But do the best you can to get as close as you can to the right size for the rower. Adjust as needed (both sneaker and rower).

Action 88: Condition of sneakers. Sneakers rip, they tear, they disintegrate into dust. A new set of sneakers, like the tracks we just discussed, can do wonders to improve rowing. Best to do this now instead of 5 minutes before launching for a race!

Having raced in many borrowed boats, Margot knows you can't always have your favourite seat in your favourite shell. She has had to deal with shoes so old they were more duct tape than shoe. They were so floppy they gave no resistance as the rate came up. She also has large feet (for a woman) and has had to scrunch her size twelves into teeny size 6 shoes. She, like many of us, knows that can be painful and distracting.

Action 89: Condition of fasteners. Check all fasteners of the sneakers and the foot stretcher. Tighten loose ones and re-place bad ones.

Action 90: Heel ties/attachments. Heel ties will loosen, disintegrate, disappear. Your mission is to make them rock solid. This step is not just about keeping referees happy at the launch dock. This is about keeping your rowers safe. Having been in more than one capsized boat we can tell you that being able to get your feet OUT of the sneakers is something you want to work every-single-time. 100%. Without failure.

Margot has noticed over many years, how many rowers (and coaches even) do not know WHY heel ties are required and important! To that point, she has written safety articles on just that piece of equipment: the rule for heel-ties 'play' is 3" or 7.5cm. (the width of a dollar bill or three fingers of "give.") Too tight and the rower cannot lift their heels, too loose and the heel tie does not give you anything to pull against.

Functioning heel ties helped this be nothing more than a "rowing experience" rather than a tragedy

Zone 4: The Riggers

A rigger supports the oar, giving it a connection to the boat so that the power put into the oar propels the boat. This means a rigger endures a lot of stress and strain. Mix that in with the terrors of travel that a rigger goes through and it is surprising that more riggers don't call in sick.

Action 91: In the right place? It's uncanny but riggers have a knack for being in the wrong place at the wrong time—and it doesn't matter how well they are marked. So a simple question, are you certain that each of your riggers are attached to the correct position in your boat? Are you a-b-s-o-l-u-t-e-l-y certain? Check manufacturer's markings or other signs that the rigger is/is not in the right place.

Action 92: Condition of rigger frame. Check the rigger's frame for issues such as cracks (especially at welds), bent stays, missing or broken fasteners. Repair and replace as needed.

Action 93: Correctly tight. After confirming riggers are placed correctly and are in good shape, tighten them correctly. Mike has videos on his YouTube channel that show how to do this effectively.

Action 94: Clean the oarlock. Turn your attention to the oarlocks. They get yucky…unbelievable so. Clean the entire thing, especially where the oar rests. While cleaning check for wear, replacing oarlocks with excessive wear and keeping a watchful eye on those that are potential candidates for future replacement.

Zone 5: The Steering

Without good steering there is no telling where the boat will end up. So, is your steering working? That's a loaded question because a human steers the boat and only some of them actually do it well. Make it easier for them by focusing on the steering mechanism and determine if it is in good condition.

Action 95: How are the cables? Steering cables will wear, even stainless steel ones. Look at the cables, especially near any friction areas. Need replacing? If so, would you rather do it now or the night before the big race (or on the launch dock — DURING the big race)? And here is another area to watch out for sharp splinters in the cables.

Action 96: Correct rudder/fin? With some boats you can have different rudders or fins for different seasons. If yours is adjustable do you have the correct one on the boat?

Action 97: Coxswain seat. The coxswain seat usually only gets attention from the coxswain. They work hard—do them a favor and make sure where they sit and work is comfortable, safe, and functional. For example, most coxswains have some variation of electronics they are dealing with. Are the holders for said electronics conveniently placed and solidly attached? A coxswain holding electronics in one hand only has one hand to steer with.

Action 98: Toe good? If the boat is toe-steered, how are the connections and cables?

Action 99: Fin straight, rudder solid? Some steering issues are not due to human error but actually to misaligned fins or broken rudders. Are they both in good working order? Turn the boat seats-down and sight along the hull to see if the fin is in line and straight. If the fin is bent can you gently straighten it? If the rudder is broken can you fix it? If in doubt or either needs replacement, reach out to the manufacturer for suggestions or parts as needed.

Takeaway

Get and then keep the boat in perfect order. Once you do so, start making the adjustments for performance, comfort and speed. (NB: Check the other books, videos and blogs in our boathouse shelf library for help. MaxRigging.com)

14

Insurance: What you don't know can hurt you, and your organization.

Bad stuff happens in the rowing world. Sometimes that bad stuff can be bad enough to require insurance. And if you don't have the proper insurance . . . well, that's a mistake you might regret for a long, long time. During downtime could be a perfect time to check that you are insurance-ready.

The day Mike became a rowing insurance fan:

Years ago one of Mike's shells, an eight, was rowing to the starting line. It was a full-buoyed course and the boat was in the assigned lane. Another crew, a four, was coming down the same lane—the wrong way! Mike's boat was in the right, the other boat was not.

None of that made any difference in the head-on-collision. At the last second, both coxswains swerved, which saved lives. But even though it was a glancing blow—it was disastrous. Mike's eight snapped completely through between the two- and three-seat. That boat sank in seconds. The four broke at the bow and went under quickly too. Fortunately there were only minor injuries, yet two shells were destroyed, oars broken, gear lost. Having the equipment insured and the athlete's insurance information handy made that terrible experience much better than it could have been.

So our question to you is if something like that happened are you insurance-ready? REALLY ready?

Here are six critical rowing areas to consider (and a prompting question to ask) from an insurance perspective:

1. Rowing equipment: What is and is not covered?

2. Launch: What must be in the launch for safety?

3. Vehicle: Who is driving and who can be in the towing vehicle?

4. Athlete health and swim ability: What are the requirements and do all the athletes meet them?

5. Coach liability: Are coaches covered for liability issues?

6. Event: Is an event you are hosting or attending covered for liability and cancellation?

Having proper rowing insurance for each of those areas could save you many headaches and a lot of money. So let us ask you five questions specific to your insurance.

(Full disclosure—WE'RE not an insurance expert and won't advise you on what coverage to get. OUR goal is to get you so excited to be insurance-ready you drop everything and call your insurance expert pronto.)

Question 1: Is your rowing equipment insurance-ready?

In Mike's accident the insurance made a world of difference. Yes, the boat and oars were replaced. But other expenses were also covered including transportation and lost belongings. Your shells and oars should be insured, and your other equipment like the electronics too. Find out if they are insurance-ready.

If they aren't, then get coverage—or be aware they aren't covered if you choose not to insure them. It's not just accidents on the water you should worry about. Here's a reality check for you…more rowing equipment is damaged in transit and storage than in any other manner. Your boathouse can be a dangerous place.

Action 100: Determine the insurance coverage of all your equipment. If you need to change insurance coverage levels (increase or decrease) contact the appropriate insurance representative.

Question 2: Is your vehicle insurance-ready?

Vehicle insurance is mandated by law almost everywhere but that doesn't mean that yours is current. Make sure the insurance is updated at least to the end of the season. Do this now because once you start back you're not going to have the time or brain power to think about this during the season.

Find the insurance cards for the tow vehicle and trailer (or your car if you're car-topping). Then put the insurance cards in the glove compartment of the tow vehicle/car, or someplace that guarantees the cards will be with the vehicle. And as an extra precaution take a picture of the cards and keep the photos on your phone.

Action 101: Determine the insurance coverage of your vehicles (truck, trailer, car, vans). If you need to change insurance coverage levels for your vehicles (increase or decrease) contact the appropriate insurance representative.

Question 3: Do you know where your athlete insurance info is?

Action 102: Confirm the insurance coverage of your athletes. Each athlete in your program should be covered by health insurance—regardless of his/her/their age group. As a coach, you'll want (and are probably expected to have) copies of your athletes' health insurance information with you in case of accident or injury, especially when traveling.

This single, smart action can save you hours of hassle.

One year, Mike had an athlete lose a fight with a bee. She was allergic, and he had to take her to emergency care. He didn't have her insurance information with him so instead of a quick doctor's visit, that missing info led to hours of hassle and filling out many other forms. He also had to pay for the visit and then spend additional time later to get reimbursed.

Today, he travels with a copy of the insurance forms for each and every athlete on the team, including the coaches. It's not a bad idea to have them for other coaches too. Mike has the info in a notebook and also has pictures of them stored on his phone.

Question 4: Do you have coach-liability insurance?

Action 103: Determine the insurance coverage of you/ coaches. Determine if YOU are covered by professional liability insurance. Few coaches take this action but the smart ones do. You may never need professional-liability coverage (and we certainly hope you don't), but if it turns out you do need it then you will REALLY need it.

We've been told by some very smart people to have at a minimum $1 million in coverage. If your program or coaching organization doesn't cover you then contact your insurance company and ask about an umbrella policy on your own insurance.

Question 5: Is your rowing event insurance-ready?

Action 104: Determine the insurance coverage for your event. If you are hosting an event then being insurance-ready is crucial. At one level or another you will want coverage (again, check with an expert on what and how much coverage you should have).

In the States, USRowing offers event coverage in specific situations, so that could be a resource for you. And event coverage can be more than for accidents. Some sporting groups had cancellation insurance coverage which they were glad to have when they had to cancel their event due to the COVID outbreak.

Save the future-you time, head space, hassles

Action 105: Keep records handy. Have records of all the above insurance coverages (and critical information) easily accessible, especially when traveling. Paper copies and digital copies both can come in extremely helpful in situations away from home.

Action 106: Questions to consider. Working on USRowing's Safety Committee we both heard many instances of accidents and injuries in our sport. Here are just a few questions that might help you conceptualize the importance of insurance and prompt you to find out more about your coverage (and if you cannot find the answers you need consider contacting an insurance company that knows rowing):

- If someone walks off the street and falls into the water off YOUR organization's dock, are you liable if they drown?
- If you have a rowing club and someone sues them, is your Board of Directors liable?
- If there is no bow ball on your organization's boat and the boat harms someone in a collision, who is covered?
- If you send out a young, inexperienced coach and there is an injury, (or worse) who is responsible?
- Is your trailer driver qualified and experienced to drive rowing equipment? And if there is an accident, do you have the coverage required?
- If a trailer is being towed by a personal vehicle, and it is damaged, is it covered, and is the organization liable?
- If your equipment is destroyed in an "act of nature" is it covered? If so, at what level?
- What swimming requirements are needed for your athletes? And do coaches need it also?

Takeaway

Insurance protects you, your equipment, and is comforting: you are being safer and wiser.

Indoor Rowers: Maximize Your Investment

15

Most rowers would rather be rowing on the water than sitting on an indoor rower. Unfortunately that's not happening for many of us right now.

If you find yourself on an indoor rower, there are numerous actions you can use to prepare the machine for your season, and in turn improve its life and performance. We are going to share five of our favorites with you.

You'll notice that the following actions are centered on the Concept2 indoor rower. That's because it is the machine we are most comfortable with. However, there are other good brands of indoor rowers available. If you have an alternative brand you may find some of these actions will be applicable to it.

Why use these actions?

We'll explain these actions in a moment but here's a distilled list of why you'll want to use them:

- To reduce the spread of illness, especially in multi-user situations
- To improve the performance of the human on the machine
- To extend the life of the machine
- To reduce injuries
- To reduce your hassles…by cutting "down-time" due to broken equipment
- To remove equipment-related barriers which can impact performance (for example, having the screen go blank with 100 meters left of a 20K).

Many of these actions will take 5 minutes or less and the supplies you need will cost less than $5 USD.

Action 107: Oil the chain. Concept2 supplies small bottles of chain oil with each new machine. You can substitute 20w oil in a pinch. Concept2 recommends you apply the oil every 50 hours of use. And it's easy to do.

Mantra

Inspect
Clean
Disinfect

Put a tablespoon of oil on a paper towel/rag, and then wipe it on the length of the chain. That's it.

Benefit: improved chain and gear life, smoother feeling during the drive

Action 108: Inspect, clean, disinfect the handle of the indoor rower. Check the handle for wear and rips in the material. Also inspect the attachment to the chain for tightness and possible frozen links.

Keep in mind that cleaning and disinfecting are two distinct and different actions as we discussed before. Cleaning is function-oriented and disinfecting is health-oriented.

Clean: The handle can get down-right gross. Sweat, grim, and oil from hands get driven into the handle each time it is rowed. Using glass cleaner, a kitchen soft scrubby, and paper towels, clean the handle frequently. Spray the handle, rub with the scrubby and then wipe dry.

After years and years of use, Margot finally realized how much she disliked the sticky feel of the old erg handle. She tried various cleaners and finally gave in, purchased a new handle from C2. And of course immediately wondered why she had suffered and endured for so long? $15. And a new handle. Easy to attach. And why did she put that off?

Disinfect: Before and after each row, disinfect the handle. There are several ways to do it. Some use disinfecting wipes, others use bleach solutions, spray or aerosols. This is critical to do in multi-user situations.

Benefit: reduced transmission of disease, reduced possibility of injury (blisters, etc), improved rower performance

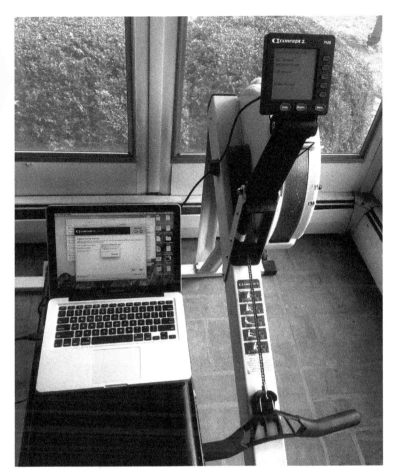

keeping your software up to date is critical

Action 109: Clean the monorail. After each practice use glass cleaner and a paper towel to clean the monorail (a.k.a. rail). We are never surprised by the amount of dirt that is removed. And it's amazing how the dirt will form bumps on the rail that make each stroke feel like driving down a pot-holed dirt road.

Benefit: improved rower performance (less resistance on monorail), less annoyance, smoother rowing.

Action 110: Keep software updated. The software for the monitors of indoor rowers are often updated. Concept2 has a free utility on its website that allows you to update your monitor. This utility allows you to:

- Update the firmware
- Upload workouts to logbooks
- Manage data on your log card or flash drive

If you have older monitors updating the firmware could be critical. It was for Mike once and he had to update multiple monitors on the same day. It will take you some time but it is well worth doing.

The specific steps are on their website, but don't hesitate to call their superior customer support line for help if needed. While on their website look for the other things you can do with your monitor, such as games and racing.

Benefit: longer life of machine, improved monitor performance, tracking of data by using logbook.

Action 111: Use wood block to stop over-compression. Over-compression happens all too often in rowing. It can cause bad technique and is a leading cause of knee injuries. And over-compression is often a habit which can be difficult for rowers to unlearn.

Here's a simple way to stop over-compression on a C2 indoor rower.

- Cut a length of 1 inch x 2 inch wood to around 10 inches in length.
- Tape the wood securely to the erg monorail. Make sure it is secure.
- Instruct rowers on how it will shorten their stroke, but will make them much more effective

This is an excellent training technique for new rowers, and when they transition to the water you can use the track's front stops to help stop over-compression there.

Benefit: reduced possibility of injury (reducing over-compression), improved rower technique, improved scores.

Action 112: Store it correctly. One of the best ways to ensure your indoor rower is ready for the upcoming season, is to store it properly when the previous season is over. Here are several important recommendations to follow before storing your machine:

1. Do use the handle hook for storage. It will not, despite common lore, cause damage. Urban myth has said it will stretch the bungee, ruin the erg. It will not.

> *Back in the Model B days when the shock cord and pulleys were all in the monorail we told people that they should not leave the handle in the handle hook because it could reduce the life of the shock cord. On the Model A's and B's if you left the handle in the handle holder there was tension on the shock cord. Once we came out with the Model C and newer where the shock cord is all up in the front end of the machine it no longer matters where you leave the handle. Even if you leave it in the handle hook there is little to no tension on the shock cord. I hope this helps.*
>
> *Greg Hammond, C2*

2. Remove batteries before storing. For rechargeable monitor models, such PM4, fully recharge the battery and then remove the battery.

3. Oil the chain and tighten loose fasteners.

4. Clean the rail.

5. Store the machine in a clean, dry location.

6. If you have a dust cover, use it…but just to protect from dust, NOT from the weather. In other words, store the machine in a clean, dry location.

And an important warning! Do not store a C2 indoor rower standing up on the front end with the two halves attached. This could cause a falling hazard that can cause injury. We've seen it happen.

> *Mike Hammond at Concept 2 said, "We don't suggest that people store the rowers upright. We prefer that they separate the monorail for storage. When they are stored together and upright it is too easy for them to be knocked over and it can be very dangerous if it fell on someone.*

It is not something we want people to do."

We have videos of several of these actions on the website (MaxRigging) and YouTube channel. They cover other preventative actions you can take, including: inspecting foot stretchers, cleaning the inside of flywheel cover, tightening fasteners and setting the drag factor. In Appendix 4 you'll also find a simple checklist of preventative actions to take for your indoor rower. And for more details on each action be sure to refer to your manufacturer's website.

Takeaway

Our message is consistent. Treat all equipment with respect and care, and keep it on the ready.

No one wants a cruddy, unresponsive rowing machine awaiting them.

Indoor Rowers Checklist

- ❏ 1. Check battery level
- ❏ 2. Update software
- ❏ 3. Clean monorail
- ❏ 4. Inspect foot stretcher
- ❏ 5. Clean foot stretcher
- ❏ 6. Inspect handle
- ❏ 7. Clean handle
- ❏ 8. Inspect seat
- ❏ 9. Oil chain
- ❏ 10. Inspect flywheel cover
- ❏ 11. Clean inside of flywheel cover
- ❏ 12. Tighten fasteners
- ❏ 13. Set drag factor

16   People: Train Your Resources

A while back, Mike was in his office. The phone rang, it was a coaching buddy, and he could hear the manic in her voice. She blurted out, "I need a trailer driver, by tomorrow! I can't find anyone anywhere!" (Implicit, she was asking if Mike would do it.)

You've probably felt that way. Obstacle. Need solution. Right Now!

That coach's options were not good:

1. Put an untrained driver behind the wheel

2. Cancel going to the event

3. Drive the trailer herself and forego some of her other duties

How did she get into this dilemma? She had not spent the time training drivers. No Plan B. She was stuck because she had no one else trained to drive. She was in a bind.

Use your downtime wisely

How do we in the 'World of Rowing' overcome challenges like this coach had? Simple, we identify a potential challenge/obstacle and make use of our downtime to Prepare the Solution. Use the downtime. Creatively.

Quality downtime in rowing is a special, important time. We're not talking about a few minutes left from a practice, or waking up in a fog at 4 a.m. We are talking about those times when you can bring clear thinking to a challenge and find a solution:

Here's an example

Continuing along with the trailering example above, how

could the coach be better prepared for the season? Well…

Action 113: Start listing your challenges. If the driver-needing coach had identified that she might/would need more than one trailer driver during the season, she could have identified a few potential people with the maturity, sense, experience and time to cultivate as potential drivers. Maybe a coach, a crew parent, or even a mechanically gifted friend. They do not NEED to be a rower!

YOU don't need to wait for an off-season to do this. Teach someone trailer driving skills on a non-racing weekend in a nearby empty parking lot. Schedule a Learn-to-Rig Party on an off-the-water day. Watch a safety video at home instead of a game show.

There are options, but you need to first identify the possible challenges ahead.

Help prepare your resources

Action 114: Your network, your resources: Can they know more? Be more useful? After the challenges are known, look at your resources: coaches, assistant coaches, parents, waterfront directors, alumni, volunteers. For any of these people to be even more helpful, they will need knowledge and training. Besides trailer driving, here are a few other areas of expertise where education can create trained specialists:

1. Launch Driving

2. Training coxswains

3. Repairing equipment

4. Rigging

5. Safety

6. Fundraising

7. Membership, Recruiting members

8. Budgeting/financial management

9. PR, newsletters

10. Events; management, volunteers

Where to start?

Action 115: Other resources. There is help out there, here are just some of the resources you can tap into:

- Online rigging courses
- Trailer driving videos
- Coaching education programs
- Coaching education newsletters
- Boating safety course
- Rowing books
- Coxswain workshops and manual

Use resources to help bring someone up to speed. And there are many more. The website of your rowing governing body may have info on many of these topics.

Locate and ask mentors

Action 116: Ask an experienced person. Margot rowed out of Potomac Boat Club (PBC) in Washington, DC for years after spending time at a club of 12 mostly-not-experienced rowers. Which meant almost none of them knew rigging or safety or many other critical pieces of information. Other rowers in local clubs were tremendously generous with their time and advice. Which did help to a large degree.

But at PBC there were some rowers who had been rowing since boarding school, and now were in their 70s. Their combined knowledge and experience was a treasure trove. Some could (and would) rig a boat for every body type, adjusting and accounting for height and strength, body irregularities, and even the hardware. The welcome recipients of this generosity would then row better, be more comfortable.

If you are rowing out of a boathouse with a large, experienced membership, plumb the depths of their know-how. If you are not, either find these sources elsewhere (perhaps a nearby coach?) or, join an online group to get advice.

Action 117: Be careful. On the job training can work, but learning under fire is a possible recipe for disaster. Examples?

- Tossing the keys to someone with no experience in driving a trailer, at the end of a long regatta day. Can they navigate corners? Handle fishtailing? Figure out how to get in and out of a gas station? Navigate overhangs?

- Someone who has never rigged a boat suddenly needs to get a boat rigged and race-ready one hour before launch. How do they know what to do?

- OR, try driving a launch for the first time while trying to coach two novice eights and avoid floating debris?

Takeaway

We have been focusing on equipment and keeping it in great shape. Do the same with your people's skills. Be ready for ALL the needs you face — train your network of support people.

1

Appendix 1
The Boathouse Checklist

Things to consider for Boathouse safety, inside and out.

Safety in the Boathouse:
- ❑ First Aid Kits
- ❑ Safety poster/reminders
- ❑ Emergency phone contact numbers
- ❑ Land line phone
- ❑ Log book (ELECTRONIC OR PAPER)
- ❑ Book to record all damages/ missing parts

Inside the Boathouse
Look around with a critical eye.

Is there any way someone could get hurt here?

Trip? Bang into something?

- Sharp edges on racks
- Slippery, oily floors
- Rags
- Riggers on the floor
- Boats in the aisles
- Misc. carts, wheels, pontoons, ergs? SPARE PARTS?
- Bottles, trash, broken glass
- Nails, screws, bolts on the floor.

Outside
The Docks and Ramps:

- Check for splintering wood or cracks.

- Broken wood pieces
- Anything slippery—
- Ice
- Bird droppings
- Moss
- Any debris:
- Trash
- Broken glass
- Fishing lures, lines and hooks

Fencing/barriers:

- NB: Your club can be liable if someone accesses your dock and comes to harm. Anyone. Not just members.
- Keep children, animals, people OFF your dock.

Make sure there are sturdy fences or barriers and signage about private property.

2

Appendix 2
The Comprehensive Trailer Checklist

☐ The shells/Boats

☐ Oars

☐ Riggers
- Tie them together, for each boat.
- Mark them to be sure they are from the correct boat and also P/S
  - Do not use duct tape to do so, it can be gummy.
  - Masking tape or Sharpies work. Or paper tape.

☐ Seats from boats and extras

☐ Tool Kit (see Appendix # 5)

☐ Extra Straps

☐ Bungees (and small ones if you bungee the seats in on the boat)

☐ Extra shoes

Red Flags

Check your regulations. There may be specifications about size and color. A small orange piece of plastic is not necessarily legal.

☐ Owner's paperwork

☐ Auto and Trailer registration

☐ Extra chain

☐ Rope

☐ List of all boats you are carrying.

If not a club boat, list owner, any existing damage, contact information and insurance. (Check and list all existing damage, so you are not held responsible later. Take photos.)

Appendix 3 Launch Checklist

3

In the US, the national governing body USRowing sells the Kippy Liddle kit, which contains:

- Telescoping 24" paddle
- Rescue Throw
- Waterproof High Intensity Flashlight
- Air Horn
- Waterproof First Aid Kit
- Emergency Blankets
- Adult USCG-Approved PFDs

Those are excellent safety tools to have with you.

Some other items to consider equipping a launch with are:

- an anchor
- bailers
- additional paddles
- rope
- fire extinguishers
- extra line
- flare kit

Depending on the size of your launch some of those items may actually be required.

On the Launch:

Does the launch have enough life jackets for every rower, coxswain and coach?

- Everyone in the launch should wear a life jacket, especially the coach.
- Keep launch lights working

• Carry VHF, FM marine radio or cell phone for communication and possible rescue

First aid kit

Tools

• Basic tool kit (see appendix #5.)
• Cell phone
• Pen and paper
• Waterproof container for tape measure, pen and paper, etc.) spare oarlocks, oar buttons and seats
• Rigger top bolts or nuts

Check:

1. Is your gas tank full?
2. Has there been any damage since your last practice?
3. Is the plug in and secure?
4. Do all lights work?
5. Is the bilge pumped out if necessary?
6. Do you have at LEAST the required number of PFDs?
7. Do you have communication to shore?
8. Is the prop clean or is it fouled by your tether line or debris?
9. Do you have at least one paddle?
10.   Are you wearing your PFD?
11.   Is the motor pumping water?
12.   Do you have:

   1. An anchor?
   2. A non verbal communication device?
   3. First aid kit?
   4. An on-the-water tool kit?
   5. Rower-specific health equipment? (such as inhaler, Epi-pen, etc.?

Appendix 4
Indoor Rower

4

Preventative Maintenance Action Checklist

- ☐ 1. Check battery level
- ☐ 2. Update software
- ☐ 3. Clean monorail
- ☐ 4. Inspect foot stretcher
- ☐ 5. Clean foot stretcher
- ☐ 6. Inspect handle
- ☐ 7. Clean handle
- ☐ 8. Inspect seat
- ☐ 9. Oil chain
- ☐ 10. Inspect flywheel cover
- ☐ 11. Clean inside of flywheel cover
- ☐ 12. Tighten fasteners
- ☐ 13. Set drag factor

5

Appendix 5
Rowing Equipment Tool Kits

Basic Rigging Tool Kit
❑ Adjustable wrenches (one large, one small)
❑ Rigger nut wrenches specific for your system
❑ Tape measure US/Metric
❑ Screwdrivers (one "+", one "-")
❑ 1 pitch meter
❑ 1 height stick
❑ Pliers
❑ Tool tray
❑ Level
❑ Hammer
❑ Utility knife (Razor blade with snap off blades)
❑ Metal file
❑ Small magnet
❑ Any wrenches specific to your shell
❑ Shims
❑ Spare hardware (nuts, washers, etc)
❑ Tapes
  ❑ Duct
  ❑ Adhesive
  ❑ Electrical
  ❑ Packing
  ❑ Masking

- ❑ Cleaning brush for oar handles
- ❑ Clean rags
- ❑ Cordless drill w bits

Travel Tool Kit

- ❑ Basic Rigging Tool Kit
- ❑ Slings
- ❑ Extra bow balls
- ❑ Extra bow clips
- ❑ Spare parts for shells and oars:
  - ❑ Pins
  - ❑ Oarlocks
  - ❑ foot stretchers
- ❑ Extra seat for each type of shell
- ❑ Extra fin, rudder and steering cable for each type of shell
- ❑ Flashlight

Basic Practice Tool Kit

- ❑ Pen and paper
- ❑ Waterproof container for tape measure, pen and paper, etc.) spare oarlocks, oar buttons and seat
- ❑ Rigger top bolts or nuts

Conclusion

Are you Water Ready?

It's time for you to put down this book and shove off the dock. Which is not, as some who aren't involved in rowing may think, an act of lunacy. Instead, it is almost always an act of passion.

What helps us accomplish that act is rowing equipment.

• Healthy, happy equipment.

• Equipment that has been prepared properly.

• Treated with respect so that it can help rowers row.

Over 100 Actions in this book will help you get your equipment, all your rowing equipment, ready to row.

And since rowing is growing and equipment changing there will be more Actions to take in the future. If you have suggestions of Actions to add here please let us know. You can reach Mike at mike@maxrigging.com and Margot at MargotZalkind@gmail.com

(For a printable list of all the Actions go to MaxRigging.com/water-ready)

We wish you a happy, healthy, safe, energetic row.

Mike & Margot

Index

CPSIA information can be obtained
at www.ICGtesting.com
Printed in the USA
BVHW011734190123
656632BV00017B/293

9 781939 767233